Landscapes of the TATRA MOUNTAINS of Poland and Slovakia

a countryside guide

Sandra Bardwell

SUNFLOWER BOOKS

First edition © 2006
Sunflower Books
PO Box 36160
London SW7 3WS, UK
www.sunflowerbooks.co.uk

Published in the USA by
Hunter Publishing Inc
130 Campus Drive
Edison, NJ 08818
www.hunterpublishing.com

ISBN 1-85691-305-8

Święty Jana Chrzciciela (Walk 8)

Important note to the reader

We have tried to ensure that the descriptions and maps in this book are error-free at press date. The book will be updated, where necessary, whenever future printings permit. It will be very helpful for us to receive your comments (sent in care of the publishers, please) for the updating of future printings.

We also rely on those who use this book — especially walkers — to take along a good supply of common sense when they explore. Conditions can change fairly rapidly in these mountains, and ***storm damage or bull-dozing may make a route unsafe at any time***. If the route is not as we outline it here, and your way ahead is not secure, return to the point of departure. ***Never attempt to complete a tour or walk under hazardous conditions!*** Please read carefully the notes on pages 30 to 39, as well as the introductory comments at the beginning of each tour and walk (regarding road conditions, equipment, grade, distances and time, etc). Explore ***safely***, while at the same time respecting the beauty of the countryside.

Cover photograph: Giewont and Kondracka Przełęcz from the Kondracka Kopa path (Walk 5)
Title page: Schronisko na Hali Ornak (Walk 7)

Photographs: the author, except for pages 4, 10, 12 (top), 22, 40, 49, 50, 69 (i-stockphoto)
Maps: John Underwood, based on the Sygnatura/Polkart and VKÚ-Harmanec maps recommended on page 31
Sunflower Books and 'Landscapes' are Registered Trademarks.
A CIP catalogue record for this book is available from the British Library.
Printed and bound in the UK by J H Haynes & Co Ltd

10 9 8 7 6 5 4 3 2 1

Contents

Ždiar (Car tour 2)

Preface

This trans-national guide explores two outstanding national parks in southernmost Poland: Pieniny and Tatra, and the best of neighbouring Slovakia's mountain areas in four national parks: Tatra, Slovenský Raj (Slovak Paradise), Low Tatra and Malá Fatra. In every one the natural landscapes are exceptionally beautiful, while each park has a distinctive identity. In the Pieniny you'll find the river Dunajec Gorge and limestone cliffs and crags. The Polish Tatra's clusters of tarns lie at the bases of spiky *arêtes,* while the adjacent Slovak Tatras are synonymous with long deep valleys and precipitous, narrow passes. Slovenský Raj has the Hornád Gorge, but the Low Tatras are characterised by spaciousness and wide views from the broad central ridge. Malá Fatra isn't entirely dissimilar, but with the added distinction of a network of narrow, accessible gorges. Beautiful conifer and deciduous forests are ubiquitous, the latter a delight during autumn.

Within the compact scope of this guide (140km east-west, 65km north-south), the contrasts between these hallmark features are striking. The two big river gorges, the broad Dunajec and the comparatively narrow Hornád, are almost vast compared with the shoulder-width slots in Malá Fatra's canyons. If these are too confined for your liking, then one of the delights of walking in the Tatra Mountains is the tumbling, boulder-filled streams. Another is the mountain tarns ranging from tiny shallow pools to the broad expanses of Morskie Oko. The vast conifer forests can seem uniform and uninteresting to the casual observer, but look closely and you quickly find infinite variety in the thick mosses, colourful fungi and extraordinary variety of lichens. The deciduous forests of beech, sycamore, mountain ash and scattered oaks are glorious during autumn. Thickets of dwarf pine, their exposed roots forming dense mats, are a characteristic feature of the uplands, as are hardy grasses and wind-pruned subalpine plants. The broad ridges and spurs of Malá Fatra, Low Tatra, Belianske and western Tatra are irresistibly inviting, while the Tatras' *arêtes* will more often be photographed than traversed.

There can be few countries where walkers are better catered for than in Poland and Slovakia. Skilfully constructed paths, often in the most improbable places high on steep-sided peaks, make walking in very rough terrain comparatively easy. You can stride across boulder fields in the High Tatra and march along the broad ridges in Malá Fatra and the Low Tatras. Old paths and trails weave through impenetrably dense forests and pine thickets. There are the unique *stúpačky* in Slovenský Raj's Hornád Gorge, and the ladders and walkways through the gorges in Malá Fatra. Four of the parks become ski resorts during winter, so you can take advantage of chair lifts, cable cars or a funicular railway and conserve energy for high-level walking. Signposting and colour-coded waymarking are almost universally excellent, so armed with this guide and with a careful eye on the waymarks, you should never be in doubt about which way to turn.

In every park you can look forward to sampling local drinks and dishes at one or more of the mountain inns. They range from the small historic Rainerova chata in the High Tatras to the large, busy *schronisko* overlooking Morskie Oko in the Polish Tatras. Generally built in harmony with their surroundings, they invariably enjoy extremely scenic, usually isolated locations and a lively, convivial atmosphere.

You'll find many and varied reminders of local history: the remains of a 13th-century castle in the Pieniny, WWII partisans' memorials in the Low Tatras, memorials to climbers at the *Symbolický Cintorín* in the High Tatras, the commemoration of a clandestine meeting between political and religious leaders in the Polish Tatras. In several towns near the mountains, especially around Zakopane, there's an abundance of beautiful wooden buildings in which people really do live. In the countryside what we may regard as outdated farming methods still involve whole families and their animals, rather than huge machines.

Language differences could make personal contacts with other walkers difficult, but you'll probably be pleasantly surprised, if my experience is any guide. I enjoyed two extraordinary conversations in French with Polish walkers, and made several attempts to explain to English-speaking Polish walkers why anyone from elsewhere in Europe would want to visit Poland. Friendly greetings are the order of the day, and it's rare not to exchange at least '*Dobry*' with passing walkers.

Walking in the national parks featured in this guide will undoubtedly be a very rewarding experience — the enjoyment of magnificent scenery and the excellent facilities for walkers, and perhaps also for successfully undertaking what may seem quite daunting walks in relatively high mountains. The experience can be rewarding in another way:

being among people who are obviously enjoying themselves, who don't seem to need an array of the latest outdoor fashions, and who are quietly proud of their mountain heritage. I hope you'll return from your visit with your appetite whetted for more.

— Sandra Bardwell

Acknowledgements
Special thanks to Barbara and Joanna in Zakopane, staff at the tourist offices in Terchová and Poprad and the national park office in Štrbské Pleso. To Pat Underwood for a treasured opportunity, to Frank and Janet for introducing me to the High Tatras, and especially to Hal for infinitely patient support and assistance.

Recommended reading

The Rough Guide to Poland by Jonathan Bousfield and Mark Salter. Excellent detailed background information on the country and its people generally and on individual towns and villages; useful practical information.

The Rough Guide to The Czech & Slovak Republics by Rob Humphreys. Another first-rate guide in every respect.

Czech & Slovak Republics by Neal Bedford, Jane Rawson, Matt Warren (Lonely Planet). Handy for practical details.

Useful contacts

For maps, guides, etc (see also Grades, waymarks, maps page 30)

www.amazon.co.uk — for travel guides and phrase books

Stanfords
12-14 Long Acre, Covent Garden, London WC2E 9LP
Tel: 020 7836 1321; www.stanfords.co.uk
e-mail:customer.services@stanfords.co.uk

The Map Shop
15 High Street, Upton upon Severn, Worcs WR8 0HJ
Tel 01684 593146; Fax: 01684 594 559; www.themapshop.co.uk
e-mail: themapshop@btinternet.com

For general information and accommodation details

Poland National Tourist Office
Westec House, West Gate, London NW5 1YY
Tel: 08700 675 010; e-mail: info@visitpoland.org

www.poland-tourism.pl, the official site of the Polish Tourist organisation, is a good source of accommodation and practical information.

Czech and Slovak Tourist Centre
16 Frognal Parade, Finchley Road, London NW3 5HG
Tel: 020 7794 3263; Fax: 020 7794 3265
e-mail: info@czechtravel.co.uk

A printed **hotel guide** (costing approximately £11 and covering all types of accommodation) is available from HEPEX-Slovakia s.r.o., Sportova 1, PO Box 32, Slovakia — 94501 Komarno. The same information is available on-line at www.travelguide.sk.

Travel

The quickest and most direct means of travel to **Poland** is by air. Scheduled flights from Britain by both mainstream and budget airlines land at Kraków, the closest airport to the areas covered in this guide. Driving to Poland from the UK takes at least two days; the distance from Calais (at the Eurotunnel exit) to the border is approximately 1000km, most directly via Belgium, Germany and into Poland on the E40 autoroute. Major international and some local hire-car companies are represented, though car hire is comparatively expensive and fuel little less so than in the UK. Bear in mind that theft of and from vehicles is common in Poland. Fly/drive and accommodation packages may be a worthwhile means of cutting down costs. State-operated trains and buses link Kraków and Zakopane, the former being slower though more comfortable; frequent local buses serve outlying towns and villages.

Air travel is also the most direct means of reaching **Slovakia**. Scheduled flights from Britain by a few mainstream and budget airlines land at Bratislava, the closest airport to the area covered in this guide. Both Vienna and Budapest are not much further away and are better served by major airlines. The drive to the western border from the UK involves more than 1000km of motorways through Belgium, southern Germany and northern Austria to Bratislava. You'll need a tax disc in Austria and Slovakia, available at the border crossing. From Bratislava, the E75/E50 motorway leads generally north nearly all the way to Žilina, on the threshold of the mountain areas. Major international and some local hire-car companies are represented, though car hire is comparatively expensive and fuel on a par with the UK. Fly/drive and accommodation packages may be a worthwhile means of cutting down costs. Excellent state-operated train services (and public and private bus lines) link Vienna and Budapest to Bratislava, and Bratislava to major towns from where frequent local buses provide good connections to the walking areas.

Indeed, public transport is so good and inexpensive in both countries that you would not be at all disadvantaged by planning a car-free holiday.

Note that citizens of western European countries, Canada and the US do not need visas to visit either country.

Car touring

There are seven car tours in this guide. Five of them outline **direct routes to the walking base(s)** in or near each of the featured national parks. Each starts from a large town with good connections to an arrival port for the relevant country, or where cars may be hired for the duration of your visit. Two of these tours offer a choice of approaches (called 'itineraries'), which could also serve as links between parks.

The two other tours describe **trans-border routes**: between Zakopane (Poland) and Poprad (Slovakia), and between Malá Fatra National Park and Zakopane. The touring routes are intended to help you plan a holiday of up to a fortnight. It's worth noting that all the routes could be linked into one extended circuit — for which you would need at least four weeks!

The tours and itineraries start and finish at places where **accommodation** is available; other places where you could stay en route are noted. For detailed information about local sights, track down the official tourist information office — called *biuro informacji turystycznej* in Poland, *informačné stredisko pre turistov* in Slovakia, as distinct from accommodation agencies, many of which display an 'Information' logo. Don't necessarily expect to find any English speakers among the staff.

Both countries' comparatively new **motorways** are built to a high standard, but **main roads** are very variable — where they're good, they're excellent, elsewhere, unpredictable. On **minor rural roads** be prepared for cavernous potholes, wandering sheep, blind corners, and horses and carts. Many Poles and Slovaks drive fast and often recklessly; they are also fond of driving while using their mobiles (although this is illegal in Poland). *Defensive driving is recommended.*

You'll always find at least one **petrol station** in large towns; in between, availability is patchy. Those in cities and larger towns in Poland are generally open daily from 6am to 10pm or longer; in rural areas most outlets are closed on Sundays. Availability in Slovakia is less generous and opening hours generally shorter. In case of a **motoring emergency**, telephone 9637 in Poland or 154 in Slovakia.

The pull-out touring map is designed to be held out opposite the touring notes and contains all the information

Štrbské Pleso (Car tours 3 and 5, Picnic 8, Walks 12 and 14)

you need on route. The key on the map explains the **symbols** used in the text. Routes via the larger towns follow the main road/highway, **bypassing the centre**. Should you choose to stop, seize the first available opportunity to park (indicated in the notes); the further you venture towards the centre, the more difficult parking becomes. Some cumulative distances and an estimated driving time are given, though the latter is likely to be confounded by road works and/or slow moving vehicles on the many long stretches where safe overtaking is impossible. If you would like additional **touring maps**, those published by Marco Polo and Sygnatura at scales of 1:200,000 or 1:100,000 are recommended.

Speed limits in both Poland and Slovakia are: in built-up areas 60km/h, on main roads 90km/h, and on dual carriage-ways 120km/h. The motorway limit is 130 km/h. However, your average touring speed is likely to be about 55km/h. You'll usually find a **café or restaurant** in towns and villages on or very close to main roads, but shopping for a picnic may be less convenient, so set out with all you'll need.

Please read the Country code on pages 33-34.

Car Tour 1: PIENINY AND TATRA NATIONAL PARKS

Two itineraries with straightforward routes to bases for walks in two Polish national parks, the first visiting a World Heritage-listed wooden church

En route: Picnics 1-7, Walks 1-10

The two Polish national parks are within easy reach of the town of Nowy Targ (84km/52mi south of Kraków). To the east a good road traverses undulating countryside, passes the large Lake Czorsztyńskie and scattered villages, most just off the road. One such is Dębno with a wonderful 14th-century wooden church (a Unesco World Heritage Site). At the small town of Krościenko, one of two possible bases for walks in Pieniny National Park, the road crosses the river Dunajec, and your route continues along a lesser road to the spa town of Szczawnica, the other base, in the rather narrow valley of the river Grajcarek.

It's only a short drive south from Nowy Targ to reach Zakopane, the gateway to Poland's Tatra National Park.

Itinerary 1: Nowy Targ • Dębno • Krościenko • Szczawnica • Nowy Targ

72km/45mi; 1h10min driving

En route: Picnics 1-2, Walks 1-3

From the dual carriageway highway 47 in **Nowy Targ** (*i* M), exit at a major junction to follow route 49 (towards *Jurgów*) back under the highway and eastwards, through two sets of traffic lights, across a bridge over the river Biały Dunajec and on to a roundabout (2.3km). Continue in the same direction along route 969 towards *Nowy Sącz*. The road leads out into the countryside in the valley of the river Dunajec, with the villages mostly set back from the road. **Dębno★** (14.5km wc), clearly signposted and on the south side of the road, is definitely worth a stop. The information boards outside the beautiful church are in Polish only, but if you happen to be there when the church is open (09.00-12.00, 14.00-16.00 Mon-Fri, 09.00-12.00 Sat), you should be able to pick up an English-language leaflet. The interior of the small church is almost completely covered in centuries-old paintings and frescoes, a miracle of preservation. Back on the main road, you soon cross the outlet from **Lake Czorsztyńskie,** then pass a junction on the left (16km) with a restaurant opposite; beside another restaurant on the same side a little further on there's a car park from which to contemplate the lake (16.4km).

Plaque at Schronisko na Chochołowskiej Polanie (Walk 8), recalling the clandestine meeting here between John Paul II and Lech Wałęsa

Above: autumn colours on the saddle below Świstowa Czuba (Walk 10); left: parish church of St Clement in Zakopane

Continuing east, past the village of **Maniowy** (19km), the road undulates gently above the lake, then climbs quite steeply from near the village of **Kluszkowce** to a viewpoint over the surrounding countryside on the north side of the road (23km). The road then begins a long descent back into the Dunajec Valley through scattered villages and farms. In the vicinity of **Połoczki** (30km) you'll find a comparative rarity in the area — a petrol station.

Continue to **Krościenko** (31.5km ; Walks 1 and 2), where, at a junction on the threshold of a bridge over the Dunajec, you continue straight ahead towards *Szczawnica*, crossing the river. The road follows the river upstream for a few kilometres to this small town, spread out just above the river Grajcarek, a tributary of the Dunajec. Most accommodation in **Szczawnica** is near the town centre (36km ; Picnics 1 and 2, Walk 3). Return to **Nowy Targ** by the same route (72km).

Itinerary 2: from Nowy Targ to Zakopane

23km/14mi; 25min driving

En route: Picnics 3-7, Walks 4-10

To leave **Nowy Targ**, head south on route 47. (If approaching Nowy Targ from the Pieniny National Park in the east, follow route 49 under the north/south highway; then turn left almost immediately towards *Zakopane,* to join the highway, route 47.) There's a petrol station almost 2km south, at the end of the dual carriageway. The busy road leads directly south, up the wide valley of the Biały Dunajec, where the villages increasingly tend to merge with each other, to the village of **Poronin** () and a major junction (17km). Continue straight on along route 47, through what could be described as not unattractive suburbs, to central **Zakopane★** (23km *i* M; Picnics 3-7, Walks 4-9).

Car Tour 2: ACROSS THE BORDER

A trans-border tour linking Zakopane, near the Polish Tatra Mountains, and Poprad, a key junction for two Slovakian parks

En route: Picnics 11-12, Walks 17-19

You soon leave Zakopane behind, following an increasingly steep, winding road through dense forest, to the border crossing at Łysa Polana. Bear in mind that this road is used by lorries heavily laden with logs, and that there are few safe overtaking opportunities. From the border you're soon travelling through completely different countryside, the broad, rolling Belianske region of the Tatra Mountains, with a scattering of attractive villages. A change of direction onto the main road through the Tatras takes you past larger settlements and on to the 'capital' of the region, Starý Smokovec, from where the major centre of Poprad in the valley below is but a short distance further on.

At Starý Smokovec the touring route intersects with Car tour 3; Poprad is the starting point for that tour and for Tours 4 and 5.

Itinerary: Zakopane • Poronin • Bukowina Tatrzańska • Łysa Polana • Tatranská Javorina • Tatranská Kotlina • Tatranská Lomnica • Starý Smokovec • Poprad

75km/46.5mi; 1h15min driving

En route: Picnics 11-12, Walks 10, 17-19

Passports required!

From the centre of **Zakopane★ (*i*⛫✝▲▲▲✕☕⛽⊕M🏞🚂🚌)** follow route 47 (Ulica Kasprowica, signposted to *Kraków*) northeast through the town's suburbs (⛽ at 4km) to the village of **Poronin** (6km ✕). Cross a bridge and, at a junction, turn right along route 961. Turn right again within 200m towards *Bukowina Tatrzańska* along Ulica Tatrzańska. The road leads generally east through settled countryside, most of the many new buildings being in the elaborate local style.

At a junction on the outskirts of **Bukowina Tatrzańska** (16km ✕), the highest village in the region, turn right along route 960 towards *Łysa Polana*. The road, not exactly highway standard and with plenty of heavy lorries, climbs steadily southwards, soon through forest. It crosses a high point at **Glodówka** (20.3km, car park) then descends, steeply in places, to **Łysa Polana** (26km ✕☕⛽).

Bear left at the junction with the road to Polana Palenica (Walk 10), pass through the **border crossing** (passport control) and continue towards *Poprad* along route 67. The road slices through a narrow valley then turns sharp right to the village of **Tatranská Javorina** (28.5km ▲▲▲✕☕⛽🚌 and shop; Picnic 12, Walk 19), clustered around a tight bend in the road. Continue, mostly through forest, to the hamlet of **Podspády** and a junction (32km). Turn right here towards *Poprad,* still along route 67. There's a parking area on the left at a tight bend (36km).

The road soon crosses a saddle and descends into open countryside and the scattered village of **Ždiar** (40km ▲▲▲✕☕⛽🚌), shown on page 4. From the

Tatranská Lomnica (Walks 17-19), with Lomnický Štít in the background (top) and the parish church at Starý Smokovec

eastern end of the village the road leads on through a forested valley to the smaller village of **Tatranská Kotlina** (47km; Walk 18). Continue to a junction (48.5km) and turn right along route 537 towards *Starý Smokovec*. The road passes through forest devastated by the storm of November 2004 (see page 91) but now recovering well, with plenty of new growth. The views of the rugged Tatra peaks, dominated by Lomnický Štít, are very impressive along here. Passing through the village of **Tatranské Matliare** () and a minor junction on the left (55km), you soon reach the attractive large village of **Tatranská Lomnica** (56.5km; Picnic 11, Walk 17). Continue along route 537, through the hamlet of **Tatranská Lesná** (59km) and on to the junction with route 534 to Poprad, at **Starý Smokovec** (62km). To reach Poprad turn left at the rail crossing. This better quality road leads directly to a major intersection on the western side of **Poprad** (75km); turn left to reach the town centre, bus and train stations. Turn right to join Car Tours 3 and 5. For Car Tour 4, follow route 18 straight on and around the southern side of Poprad.

Car Tour 3: SLOVAKIA'S TATRA MOUNTAINS

Eastwards through the Tatras mountain villages and small towns, starting and finishing in Poprad

En route: Picnics 8-10, Walks 11-16

From Poprad you first drive westwards to the village of Tatranská Štrba (which happens to be on a major geographical divide between east- and west-flowing European rivers). Here, leave the busy highway to drive up to the resort of Štrbské Pleso, the base for some of the Tatra National Park walks. The main 'High Tatras' road winds generally eastwards across the steep mountainsides, through several villages and areas affected by the November 2004 storm (see page 91), to the colourful small town of Starý Smokovec, the second base for High Tatras walks. Poprad is only a short distance south down a busy wide road.

Itinerary 1 of Car Tour 5 (to the Low Tatras National Park) leads west from near Štrbské Pleso; at Starý Smokovec, the route of Car Tour 3 intersects with that of Car Tour 2.

Itinerary: Poprad • Tatranská Štrba • Štrbské Pleso • Starý Smokovec • Poprad

50.5km/31mi; 1h driving

En route: Picnics 8-10, Walks 11-16

From **Poprad** (*i*✝⊕M) join route 18, which skirts the town to the south and southwest, and follow it westwards. It goes through the mainly industrial town of **Svit** (8km) and past the junction of route 539 (to Vyšné Hágy on the main High Tatras road). On reaching **Tatranská Štrba** (18km Δ), turn right along route 538 which leads through the village then winds steeply up in a series of tight bends to a junction with route 537, the 'High Tatras' road (25km).

Turn right; then, 0.5km further on, go left towards *Štrbské Pleso*. The resort of **Štrbské Pleso** (*i*⊕; Picnics 8 and 9, Walks 11-14) is 1.5km up the winding road; see plan on the reverse of the touring map for the location of parking areas.

To continue to Starý Smokovec, follow route 537 eastwards (signposted to *Smokovece*— the three adjacent settlements of Nový Smokovec, Starý Smokovec and Horný Smokovec), along a comparatively tortuous stretch of road, then through the village of **Vyšné Hágy** (30.5km). A parking area on the right (32km) affords a view southwards, across admittedly storm-damaged forest; there's a similar view from another parking area beyond the nearby village of **Nová Polianka** (33km). The road passes through two more villages, then comes to **Nový Smokovec** (36.5km) from where it's only a short distance further to **Starý Smokovec** (37.5km ✝⊕; Picnics 10-12, Walks 15-19; photographs opposite and page 88). **Horný Smokovec** () is 1km further east along route 537.

At the eastern end of Starý Smokovec you'll find the junction of routes 537 and 534, the road back to **Poprad** (50.5km).

Car Tour 4: SLOVAK PARADISE

A circular tour to and from the enticingly-named Slovak Paradise National Park, visiting a fine old walled town en route.

En route: Picnics 13-14, Walks 20-22

This tour starts and finishes in the large, bustling town of Poprad. It follows the busy highway (E58/18) eastwards, mostly a two-lane road thronged with lorries (Košice, Slovakia's prosperous second city, approximately 100km to the east, accounts for much of this traffic), to the old walled town of Levoča. Exploring the town centre, with several well-preserved medieval buildings, is well worth a couple of hours. From there drive south towards the largish town of Spišská Nová Ves, more of a commercial centre than a tourist destination. It can easily be bypassed to reach the dispersed hamlet of Čingov on the threshold of Slovenský Raj (Slovak Paradise) National Park. The return to Poprad passes through undulating countryside of large fields and compact villages to rejoin the highway at Spišský Štvrtok, east of Poprad.

Poprad is a major touring junction for this guide: it's at the southern end of Tour 2 from Zakopane in Poland, the start and finish of Tour 3 to the Tatra National Park, and the point from where you could drive west to join Tour 5 to the Low Tatras National Park or Tour 6 to Malá Fatra.

Itinerary: Poprad • Spišský Štvrtok • Levoča • Spišská Nová Ves • Čingov • Spišské Tomášovce • Spišský Štvrtok • Poprad

65km/39mi; 1h10min driving

En route: Picnics 13 and 14, Walks 20-22

From **Poprad** (i✝⛪▲✕☕⛽⊕M 🚂🚌) set out along the E50/18, the major highway which skirts the southern side of the town, leading eastwards towards *Levoča*. Beyond the newer medium-rise housing on the right, the road traverses undulating countryside, with generally large fields and compact villages. There are

Spišské Tomášovce from Pri Tomáš Výhľade (Walk 20)

Levoča: Thurzo House, (top) and the town hall

'motorests' (✕) at the villages of **Hôrka cast Kosovce** (7.5km, on the south side of the road) and at **Hôrka cast Hôrka** (8.5km, on the north side).

Continue along the highway at a major junction in **Spišský Štvrtok** (15km ▲■⛽🚌); attractively tree-lined, it climbs through hilly country then descends into the valley sheltering the town of Levoča, passing the Starý Mlyn 'motorest' (22km ✕⛽) en route. Follow the highway up into **Levoča★** (26km *i*⛫✝▲▲✕■⛽⊕M🚌); there is a signposted parking area on the left opposite a large hospital. Walk up the road for about 150m to enter the walled town through the Košice gate.

Exit from the parking area and turn right. Turn left 1km further on, along route 533 towards *Spišská Nová Ves*. The road leads quite directly south down a narrow valley, through the village of **Harichovce** (32.5km ✝✕■) and on across the defunct railway line. At a junction (34.5km ⛽), turn right, still along the 533. Within 0.6km you can diverge to the left to follow route 536 which bypasses the centre of **Spišská Nová Ves** (36km *i*✝▲▲✕■⛽⊕🚂🚌). Unless you are stopping here, continue west on route 536, through the 'suburb' of **Smižany**. On coming to a junction (39km), turn left and follow the minor road (initially a residential street) under the railway and past another junction on the left. At the next junction (40km), turn right to **Čingov** (▲✕■🚌). The main hotels are 1.2km further along on the left.

To return to Poprad, continue along the road from Čingov to a junction (41.7km) where the national park entrance is nearby to the left. Turn right here; the road winds around and down to the village of **Spišské Tomášovce** (▲✕ and shop). Turn right at a junction (43.3km) and follow the road — across the railway, around a series of sharp bends, and on to the main road from Spišská Nová Ves (route 536; 46.3km). Turn left and go on to **Spišský Štvrtok** (▲■⛽🚌), where you meet the highway (E50/18; 50.3km). Turn left to return to **Poprad** (65km).

Car Tour 5: LOW TATRAS NATIONAL PARK

A choice of routes to the gateway town of Liptovský Mikuláš and a straightforward drive on to the resort of Jasná

En route: Picnics 8, 9, 15, 16; Walks 11-14, 23-25

Two routes to Liptovský Mikuláš are outlined; the first is straightforward — west from Poprad through the wide Poprad and Vah valleys along major highways. The second route provides a direct link with the Tatra National Park tour (Car Tour 3), via the more western reaches of the Tatra Mountains and the Vah Valley. From Liptovský Mikuláš, a pleasant town with an attractive pedestrianised centre, it's a short direct drive south along a generally good road through the forested, narrow Demänová Valley, to the resort of Jasná, the base for walks in the national park.

You can continue west from Liptovský Mikuláš, following Itinerary 1 of Car Tour 6, to Malá Fatra National Park.

Itinerary 1: Poprad • Tatranská Štrba • Liptovský Hrádok • Liptovský Mikuláš

59.5km/37mi; 1h driving

From **Poprad** (*i* ✝ ⊕ M) follow route 18, the main road westwards which skirts the town to the south and southwest. It runs through the mainly industrial town of **Svit** (8km). You pass the junction with route 539 (to Vyšné Hágy on the main High Tatras road) and come to

Vrbické Pleso, near Jasná (Picnic 15, on Intinerary 3)

Tatranská Štrba (18km Δ ✕) — and the junction with route 538 towards Štrbské Pleso (see Car Tour 3). Continue westwards, then pick up the D1 motorway near the small town of **Važec** (24km). Continue along the D1; there's a motorest at **Hybe** (36km ✕). Then, at a major junction with route 537 (44km), leave the D1 in the direction of *Liptovský Hrádok*. Drive through **Liptovský Peter** to **Liptovský Hrádok** (✕), where you come to another major junction. Turn right along route 18 and continue through the town, under the motorway and on to **Liptovský Mikuláš** (59.5km *i* ✕ ⊕ M).

Itinerary 2: Štrbské Pleso • Podbanské • Liptovský Hrádok • Liptovský Mikuláš

45.5km/28mi; 1h driving

En route: Picnics 8 and 9, Walks 11-14

From **Štrbské Pleso** drive down the access road to the junction with route 537 (1.5km) and turn right. The road follows a fairly straightforward route, generally downhill, across the steep moun-

Church of St Nicholas, Liptovský Mikuláš

tainsides. At the time of writing the several parking areas beside the road (), most of which afford views southwards across the valley below, were occupied by piles of logs awaiting removal. Hopefully you will be able to park for the views.

It's worth stopping at the first village you pass, **Podbanské** (15.5km), if only for the awesome view of the peak Kriváň to the northeast (Walk 14). Podbanské is at the western extremity of the storm-affected forest (see page 91). The road turns southwest here, leaves the Tatra National Park and soon emerges into lightly wooded agricultural countryside, particularly beautiful during autumn. Just before the village of **Pribylina** (24.5km) there's a hotel beside the **Museum of the Liptov Village**, featuring local architecture, on the right (**M**). Continue past **Vavrišovo** (29.5km Δ) to a major junction with the D1 motorway (31.5km). Drive under the motorway and go on through **Liptovský Peter**, then the larger town of **Liptovský Hrádok** (34.5km). On reaching another major junction, turn right along route 18 and continue through the town, under the motorway and on to **Liptovský Mikuláš** (45.5km *i* M).

Itinerary 3: Liptovský Mikuláš • Jasná • Liptovský Mikuláš

31km/19mi; 40min driving

En route: Picnics 15 and 16, Walks 23-25

From the centre of **Liptovský Mikuláš** (*i* M) drive southwest along a dual carriageway for 1km to a major intersection with the D1 motorway. Follow signs for *Jasná* to reach route 584. The road passes through the village of **Demänová** then runs briefly through open countryside, past a junction on the right (6km Δ) and into the deep, forested **Demänová Valley** (). Two large caves close to the road are open for guided visits (Tues-Sun): **Demänovská L'adova Jaskyňa**, a huge ice cave (8km) — take plenty of warm clothing! and **Demänovská Jaskyňa Slobody**, the 'Cave of Freedom' used by World War II partisans (10.5km).

Beyond the latter the road climbs, steeply in places, past **Záhradky** (13.5km; Picnic 16) and on to **Jasná**, more a dispersed group of hotels and skiing facilities than a true village (15.5km *i* ; Picnic 15, Walks 23-25; see map pages 108-109).

For the return to **Liptovský Mikuláš**, there's no alternative to retracing your outward drive (31km).

Car Tour 6: MALÁ FATRA

Two itineraries to Terchová, gateway for the Malá Fatra National Park, one from other parks to the east, the other from the south

En route: Picnics 17-20, Walks 26-31

Malá Fatra, the westernmost park featured in this guide, can be reached by an interesting route from the east, or from the south if you travel from Bratislava (approximately 160km to the south), or even Prague. From the east you leave the busy highway (E50/18) at the village of Strečno, to visit the local castle — literally perched on a bluff directly above the sinuous river Vah. Then, to bypass the town of Žilina, you cross the river on an unusual 'ferry' and continue via the small town of Varín to the main Žilina/Terchová road. From Žilina the route is quite direct, along a regional road through increasingly hilly countryside and a string of rather plain small towns to Terchová.

The drive between Liptovský Mikuláš, the centre for Car Tour 5, and Terchová is partly along the D1 motorway. This has three advantages over the less direct route 18: it's elevated above the surrounding countryside, it runs along the southern shore of the attractive lake Liptovská Mara, and the quality of the road surface is better. From the end of the D1, back on route 18, you pass through several industrial towns and through two quite impressive small gorges on the river Vah.

From Terchová you could simply retrace your route to the highway to reach your next destination. Alternatively, if your next port of call happens to be Poland, then Car Tour 7 is a convenient (although not exhilaratingly scenic) route to the Polish border, from where it's not far to Zakopane.

Ferry across the Vah, near Strečno

Itinerary 1: Liptovský Mikuláš • Ružomberok • Kral'ovany • Strečno • Varín • Terchová

93km/58mi; 1h20min driving

En route: Picnics 17-20, Walks 26-31

From a major junction on route 18 in central **Liptovský Mikuláš** (*i* ⛰⛺✕⛽⊕M🚂🚌) a clearly signposted road provides access to the D1 motorway — follow signs for *Žilina*.

At **Dechtáre** (8km ✕📷) there's a good opportunity to park directly above the shore of **Liptovská Mara**. The motorway ends beyond the western extremity of the lake, near **Ivachnova** (16km ✕⛽), from where route 18/E50 leads on westwards.

Soon you reach the outskirts of the large town of **Ružomberok** (22km *i* ⛰⛺✕⛽⊕🚂🚌), passing large cooling towers and other industrial sites. There's no special reason to linger here, so continue along route 18, past the junction of route 59/E77 in the town centre. The **Vah Valley** closes in, with the road closely following the river's sinuous course. There's a parking area on the crest of a wide bend (30.5km), then you drive through the villages of **Hubová** (33km ⛰✕) and **L'ubochňa** (35km ✕), where you'll find a restaurant a short distance to the left, off the main road.

The road crosses the river at **Kral'ovany** (40km ⛺✕), just below its confluence with the **river Orava**. On coming to a junction, turn left towards *Žilina*. The road winds around a U-bend then traverses a wide section of the valley, through unremarkable small towns (each with a petrol station; ⛽), crosses the river again, passes the large town of **Martin** (59km) and returns to the river-side. The Vah flows through another narrow gorge; there are parking areas at 66km and 69.5km (📷 on the apex of another U-bend), from which to better appreciate the spectacle.

The road soon passes close to Strečno Castle, but to reach the castle when travelling west, you must first leave route 18 and go to a junction in **Strečno** (73.5km *i* ⛺✕📷🚌), from where the castle is clearly signposted. Soon you turn right at an intersection and follow the road through the village, beside the river, past a coffee shop and under the highway, to a parking area beside a bar-restaurant (75.5km).

The steps for the first part of the climb to **Strečno Castle** ★ (▮) are to your right. From the top of the steps, follow an unsurfaced road past a block of plain buildings to a cobbled road leading up to the castle entrance. To see inside this 14th-century 'National Cultural Monument' you'd need to participate in a guided tour, which may well not be available for English speakers. However, the views from the ramparts are spectacular, and you can learn something of its history from information boards here.

To continue towards Terchová and to bypass the large town of Žilina, drive back towards Strečno village for approximately 250m (almost as far as the coffee shop), to a minor road on the right. This leads to the small 'Kompa' cable ferry across the river Vah. It operates on demand rather than to a set timetable.

On the far side, in the village of **Nezbudská Lúčka** (75.8km ✕), turn left along a minor road. It parallels the river and railway, crosses the latter and leads on close to the river, but without any views. The road bends to the right, away from the river, into the outskirts of the small town of

Varín (77.8km). It then bears left across the **river Varínka**. About 0.3km further on, beyond a large church and along a cobbled road, it enters a small square. Turn right along a wide street and follow it through the town to the main Žilina/Terchová road, route 583 (80km).

Turn right; the road passes through a handful of large villages, the turnoff to a hotel on the right (88.2km), a camping ground beside the road on the left (89.3km Δ) and on past the local petrol station (91.3km) to **Terchová**★ (93km *i* ⊕M).

Itinerary 2: Žilina • Teplička • Terchová

24km/15mi; 20min driving

En route: Picnics 17-20, Walks 26-31

From **Žilina** (*i* ⊕) follow route 18 through the town, generally northeastwards (if coming from Bratislava) to a major junction on the northern side of the bridge over the **river Vah**.

Turn right along route 583 towards *Terchová*. The road leads eastwards across the flat valley, through the small town of **Teplička** (5km), past fields and occasional factories. Stay on the main road past junctions on the right to Varín (Itinerary 1 joins at the second of these junctions; 11km).

The road then turns northeastwards into the narrower **Varínka Valley**, flanked on the right by fields, with steep wooded mountainsides beyond. The road runs through a handful of large villages and passes the turn-off to a hotel on the right (19.2km), a camping ground beside the road on the left (20.3km Δ) and the local petrol station (22.3km), before coming into **Terchová**★ (24km *i* ⊕M).

Orava Castle (Car tour 7)

Car tour 7: ORAVA VALLEY

From Terchová across the border to the Polish Tatra Mountains

En route: Picnics 3 and 4, Walks 7 and 8

This tour links the Malá Fatra National Park (Car tour 6) with Zakopane, the base for Poland's Tatra National Park. The greater part of the route is along a busy road through the wide Orava Valley, scenic in places, but blighted by a few gruesome industrial sites and unsightly blocks of apartments in a couple of towns. It's not until you've crossed the border at Suchá Hora that things improve, in the nearby village of Chochołow, a living museum of wooden houses. Soon you're driving through Zakopane's satellite villages.

Itinerary: Terchová • Párnica • Dolný Kubín • Tvrdošín • Trstená • Suchá Hora • Chochołow • Zakopane

95km/57mi; 1h50min driving

En route: Picnics 3, 4, Walks 7, 8

Passports required!

Head east from **Terchová** () along the main 583 road. Beyond the hamlet of **Biely Potok** (), climb steeply to a pass, **Sedlo Rovná Hora** (5km), then descend to an intersection (8km). Turn right, still on route 583, and follow it south down the narrow, steep-sided and forested valley past the village of **Lučivňa** (13.3km) to a junction at **Párnica** (16.5km) in the **Orava Valley**. Turn left on route 70 towards *Dolný Kubín*. In the small town of **Veličná** the road makes a sharp left turn and leads on to a major junction in the town of **Dolný Kubín** (25.5km). Turn left towards *Trstená* along route 59/ E77. Just beyond the grim industrial town of **Široká** (31.5km), roadworks may cause a hold-up.

Orava Castle★ (), on top of a cliff above **Oravský Podzámok** (34km), dates from the 13th century and is one of the most intact in Slovakia. To visit, turn right to the car park in the village centre and join the obligatory guided tour (but check first about English translations!).

Beyond **Sedliacka Dubová** (41km), some older houses in the village of **Dlhá nad Oravou** () make it more attractive than most in the area. The small town of **Podbiel** (48km) is unusual for this valley, in that it modestly caters for visitors. The road crosses the river (51km), passes through the small town of **Nizná**, then larger **Tvrdošín** (55km), which almost merges with **Trstená** (61km). Towards the northern end of town, turn right along route 520 towards *Suchá Hora*.

This quieter road leads east through a wide valley, with plain villages strung out on either side. It crosses a low ridge, then climbs again past Hladovka and on through **Suchá Hora** () to the **border crossing** (76km ; passport control; exchange). Continue straight on along route 959, to a junction in the village of **Chochołow** (77km), notable for its many fine 19th-century wooden houses and public buildings; a small museum is devoted the local uprising against the Austrians in 1846. Turn right here on route 958. Drive through the village of **Witów** (), then a belt of forest. You pass the turn-offs to the Chochołowska and Kościeliska valleys and continue through increasingly settled countryside to **Zakopane★** (95km).

Picnics and short walks

River banks, lakesides, scenic lookouts, meadows, and mountain inns all offer opportunities for dining outdoors. Formal picnic grounds, with tables and other facilities, or benches beside rivers and so on, are quite common in both Poland's and Slovakia's national parks, but it would still be prudent to take something to sit on, since picnicking is very popular and all the amenities may be occupied!

All the picnic spots recommended in this section are easy to reach; some follow parts of the walks described elsewhere, others are fine short walks in their own right. None is more than 50 minutes from a safe parking place or public transport, though the majority are much closer; remember that the times shown are out *and back*.

The location of each picnic is shown by the symbol ***P*** printed in green on the relevant walking or touring map, and some are illustrated. The symbol ○ indicates a site in full sun. **Keep in mind the Country Code on pages 33-34.**

Stock up with oven-fresh rye bread, some spicy salami, *oscypki* (the ubiquitous smoked goats' cheese, on sale at street stalls), pickled cabbage, fresh cucumber and tomatoes, stone fruit, locally-grown apples or plums from an outdoor market, a bottle of local beer or wine — what more could you ask!

1 Sokolica ridge *(map pages 42-43)*

🚘 (Car tour 1). 🚌: see transport for Walk 2 on page 133. 1h30min on foot, with approximately 25m/82ft ascent. Follow Walk 2 to the 45min-point; picnic on the grass; retrace steps to the start.

After crossing the river Dunajec by punt, a short climb leads to a meadow with attractive views of part of the small town of Szczawnica.

2 Dunajec Gorge *(map pages 42-43; photograph page 49)*

🚘 (Car tour 1). 🚌: see transport for Walk 3 on page 133. 1h on foot, with negligible ascent. Starting from the car park at the confluence of the rivers Grajcarek and Dunajec, follow Walk 3 from the 23min-point to the 49min-point; retrace steps from there. Take advantage of the picnic table close to the Lesnica road junction.

A quiet road offers an introduction to the spectacular Dunajec Gorge.

3 Gubałówka ○ *(touring map, and partly shown on the plan of Zakopane on the reverse of the touring map; photograph opposite)*

(Car tours 1 and 7). from Zakopane to Gubałówka (see Transport, page 132). The nearest convenient car park is beside Ulica Nowotarska, just north of the intersection with Ulica Krupówki to the east and Droga na Gubałówkę to the west: walk up the latter, under the highway and up to the funicular station). 55min on foot, all downhill (approximately 220m/722ft). Exit from the upper funicular station and turn right along the road (used only by local people). It soon bends left past a communications tower and descends to an unsurfaced road on the right (16min); follow blue waymarks from here. Bear left along a track past a house with distinctive dormer windows (24min) and continue to the forest ahead. A trail leads straight on, then across a small meadow,

Picnic 3 (optional side-trip): wooden church at Gubałówka

through a narrow band of trees, to a large meadow with excellent mountain views (40min), where you can picnic on the grass. From the far side of the meadow, bear left downhill, more or less on the edge of the field. The path then swings right into a narrow valley for about 200m to meet a trail, which you follow to the right. It becomes an unsurfaced road between houses, then a narrow road that leads down to a junction; turn right across a bridge, back to the lower funicular station (55min).

Optional side-trip or Alternative shorter walk From the upper funicular station exit, turn *left* along the road for 0.5km, to the pretty wooden church shown on page 25, set back from the road on the right; there are benches under the mountain ash trees in its grounds.

An outstandingly scenic downhill walk through some of Zakopane's rural hinterland with unrivalled panoramic views of the Tatra Mountains.

4 Zakopane's meadows *(map pages 52-53)*

(Car tour 1) or (minibus) to the Strążyska Dolina car park and back, as Walk 4 on page 51. 20min on foot. Follow Walk 4 along Droga pod Reglami, at the edge of the forest, with fine views across meadows to Zakopane. Picnic on the grass, or take advantage of the numerous benches shaded by the tall conifers.

Enjoy peace and quiet and fine views of Gubałówka and Zakopane only 10 minutes' drive from the town centre.

5 Schronisko Kalatówki *(map pages 52-53)*

(Car tour 1); park on the outskirts of Zakopane (the nearest car park to Kuźnice is very small; it's beside the road, near the junction of Ulica P Tatrzańskich and Ulica M Karłowicza, 1km north of Kuźnice). from Zakopane: take either No 1 or No 5 on the regular service, or private minibus from opposite the bus station; return by private minibus (see transport for Walk 5 on page 133). 1h on foot, with 173m/567ft ascent. Follow Walk 5 (page 55) to the 30min-point, at a meadow dominated by the large refuge, Schronisko Kalatówki. From here you can see the buildings at the top of the cable car station far above to the southeast. Picnic on the grass or try the buffet at the inn.

To the threshold of the high mountains, with views towards the Poland-Slovakia border ridge.

6 On the Poland-Slovakia border ○ *(map pages 52-53, photograph page 57)*

(Car tour 1); see Picnic 5 above re parking and buses from Zakopane to Kuźnice. Then from Kuźnice to Kasprowy Wierch (see Transport on page 132). 30min on foot, with approximately 40m/131ft ascent. From the upper cable car station exit follow the broad paved trail gently downhill, to an unsignposted junction in a shallow saddle. Turn left to follow a well-used, red-waymarked trail, up and along the ridge to the rocky summit of Beskid (2012m). Retrace steps to the start. You should be able to find a quiet picnic spot not too far from the cable car station (on the high ground to the right — the summit of Kasprowy Wierch); alternatively, descend a little way from Beskid towards the grassy saddle further east along the ridge. Please see the note on page 32 about the 'Effects of altitude'.

The easy way to enjoy outstanding mountain vistas — by cable car to Kasprowy Wierch, almost on the border.

7 Polana Huciska ○ *(map pages 64-65, nearby photograph pages 62-63)*

(Car tour 1) to Siwa Polana: from Zakopane follow route 958 (Ulica Nowotarska and Ulica Kościeliska) generally south and west to the minor road signposted 'Dolina Chochołowska' (7km); turn left to the car park on the left (7.9km). from opposite Zakopane bus station to Siwa Polana (see transport for Walk 7 on page 133). From the national park entrance, a 'bus' (a dressed-up tractor pulling two carriages) plies the valley road as far as Polana Huciska (3.5km); costing only pence, it runs half-hourly from 08.00. Alternatively, horses and open carriages, their drivers in traditional garb, also operate along the road, though for a larger fee. Another possibility is to hire a cycle at Siwa Polana, ride to Polana Huciska and back, or return the cycle at Polana Huciska and walk back. 45min on foot, slightly downhill. Reach Polana Huciska by 'bus', carriage or cycle for a picnic on the grass, or at one of the picnic tables or benches, then walk back to Siwa Polana.

A gentle introduction to the most extensive of the valleys reaching into the mountains near Zakopane, by rustic bus, cycle or on foot.

8 Štrbské Pleso *(map pages 74-75 and plan on reverse of the touring map; photographs pages 10, 74)*

(Car tours 3 and 5); park in Štrbské Pleso village. Or or to Štrbské Pleso (see transport for Walk 11 on page 133). 45min on foot, with negligible ascent. Start from the signposted intersection near the post office (see plan): follow the minor road to the left, past the huge Hotel Hviezdoslav, to a signposted intersection opposite the entrance to imposing Liečebný Dom Solisko. Continue by following blue waymarks across open ground between the hotel and the lake shore. A paved path to the left then leads onwards, shortly passing a tiny peninsula (benches, war memorial), then along a track, with Chata pod Soliskom and the striking peak of Kriváň in view (Walks 12, 14). Pass a junction with the path to/from Chata pod Soliskom (Walk 13) on the left (20min). Beyond an oddly-shaped hotel there are more good views of Kriváň and Mlynická Dolina (Walk 13), near where a red-waymarked path leads left to the main village road near the Hotel Helios junction. The surface soon changes to tarmac at some tennis courts and continues thus to a plaque dedicated to Jozef Szentiványi, prominent in the lake's beginnings as a health resort. From here bear left along a path; then go left again, parallel with a road, to emerge near the start on your right.

Magnificent mountain views from a popular path around a beautiful lake with plenty of picnic benches along the shore.

9 Predné Solisko *(map pages 74-75, photograph page 77)*

, or as Picnic 8, then chair lift from Štrbské Pleso village (see transport for Walk 12 on page 133). 1h5min on foot, with approximately 253m/830ft ascent. Follow Shorter walk 12-1 on page 76 from Chata pod Soliskom up to the summit of Predné Solisko and back.

After a breathtaking chair lift ride, climb to an easily accessible summit for superb views across Štrbské Pleso village to the lowlands, then enjoy drinks at the chata below.

10 Rainerova Chata *(map pages 86-87)*
🚗 (Car tours 2 and 3), 🚂 or 🚌 to Starý Smokovec, then 🚋 funicular railway from Starý Smokovec to Hrebienok (see transport for Walk 15 on page 133). 45min on foot, with approximately 80m/260ft ascent. Follow Shorter walk 15-1 on page 84 to Rainerova Chata and back.
An excellent introduction to the central High Tatras, with some tantalising mountain views and a visit to the most atmospheric and homely of the chatas *in the national park.*

11 Veľká Lomnická Veža ○ *(map pages 86-87)*
🚗 (Car tour 2), 🚂 or 🚌 to Tatranská Lomnica, then 🚡 cable car to Skalnaté Pleso (see transport for Walk 17 on page 134). 25min on foot, with approximately 115m/380ft ascent. Follow Short walk 17 on page 90.
A spectacularly scenic short ridge walk below Lomnický Štít, the most striking landmark peak in the High Tatras.

12 Pod Muráňom ○ *(map page 96; nearby photograph page 97)*
🚗 (Car tour 2) or 🚌 to Tatranská Javorina (see transport for Walk 19 on page 134). 56min on foot, with approximately 80m/262ft ascent. Follow Walk 19 to the 28min-point at Pod Muráňom, with picnic tables.
Follow a forest trail in the eastern Belianske Tatras to a delightful meadow, dramatically overlooked by the massive white limestone walls of a huge bluff.

13 Beside the river Hornád *(map page 102)*
🚗 (Car tour 4) or 🚌 to Podlesok (see transport for Walk 21 on page 134). 56min on foot, with minimal ascent. Follow Walk 21 to the 28min-point. Picnic on the nearby grassy banks of the river; retrace steps to Podlesok.
A tranquil riverside picnic near the entrance to the exciting traverse of the Hornád Gorge.

14 Between Čingov and Masa ○ *(map page 102)*
🚗 (Car tour 4) or 🚌 (see transport for Walk 20 on page 134) to Čingov, then on foot. 40min, with approximately 50m ascent. Start at a junction on the Čingov/Spišská Nová Ves road, at the top of a small steep rise 300m east of the road junction leading into Slovenský Raj National Park. Follow the minor road, signposted to two hotels, past the Čingov Hotel and on to the entrance to the Park Hotel. Turn right here to join a wide path about 30m away and distinguished by a yellow waymark on a tree. Follow the waymarked path through forest, to emerge suddenly on grassland. Continue with yellow poles to the right, across grassland just below the crest on your left. When the path starts to descend, diverge left up the slope to the crest for a panoramic view of the area. For an excellent vista of the village of Masa and the mouth of the Hornád Gorge, return to the path and continue downhill for a few minutes. Picnic on the grass.
Varied wide views of wooded ranges, villages and the Hornád River from a lookout near Čingov.

15 Vrbické Pleso *(map pages 108-109, photograph page 18)*
🚗 (Car tour 5) or 🚌 to Jasná (see transport for Walk 23 on page 134). 25min on foot, with negligible ascent. From the bus stop or adjacent car park walk up the road to the right of Hotel Grand for about 20m, to a trail on the right. Go down this, to a notice board. Turn right up a trail through conifers to a junction beside a log bridge on the shore of

Vrbické Pleso. Turn left to start a circuit; the trail parallels the shore, passing several picnic benches. The best view materialises almost immediately, up to the main Low Tatras ridge. After about 10min, turn right at a junction, to a picnic table and benches on a small peninsula. Continuing along the main trail, 2min further on climb a few steps and turn right. Soon you come to a bench on the right with another good view of the ridge. Not much further along, bear right along a yellow-waymarked path, shortly passing a vista of the long spur extending north from the ridge (beside an information board in Slovak). Continue to the log bridge nearby, and turn left to return to the start.
An exceptionally scenic circuit of a beautiful lake near Jasná with good vistas of the high central ridge.

16 Chopok *(map pages 108-109, photograph pages 112-113)*

(Car tour 5) or to Záhradky near Jasná, then two chair lifts to Chopok Úboč (see transport for Walk 24 on page 134). 1h on foot, with 364m/1194ft ascent. Follow Shorter walk 24-1 (page 111) from and back to the top chair lift station.
An ascent of one of the highest peaks in the Low Tatras, with an excellent chata *nearby— try their sweet dumplings.*

17 Chleb ○ *(map page 120, photograph page 118)*

(Car tour 6) or to Chata Vrátna, then chair lift (from Terchová, see transport for Walk 27 on page 134). 58min on foot, with approximately 146m/479ft ascent. Follow Shorter walk 27-1 from the chair lift terminus up to Snilovské Sedlo and on to the summit of Chleb (1646m). Picnic among the surrounding rocks. Retrace steps to the chair lift.
Take advantage of a chair lift to make an easy ascent of a peak on the central Malá Fatra ridge.

18 Chata na Grúni *(map page 120)*

or as Picnic 17 above. 1h30min on foot, with 220m/722ft ascent. Start just uphill from the bus stop at Chata Vrátna and turn left in front of the *chata* entrance along a yellow-waymarked path. It's a perfectly straightforward route along a mostly well-graded path. You wind around a small valley, cross a spur, then head up a valley to Chata na Grúni — in a wide meadow below the ridge forming the spine of Malá Fatra. The menu (drinks, snacks, meals) is in Slovak and German. Retrace steps to Chata Vrátna.
An easy walk to a superbly-sited chata, *for the best cappuccino in Slovakia's mountains.*

19 Koliba Podžiar *(map page 124)*

(Car tour 6) or to Štefanová from Terchová (see transport for Walk 30 on page 134). 54min on foot. Follow Walk 30 on page 127 from Štefanová to the 27min-point at Koliba Podžiar; retrace steps to Štefanová.
Refreshments at a rustic log cabin surrounded by impressive rocky peaks rising above steep forested slopes.

20 A Slovak hero's walk ○ *(map page 129, photograph page 130)*

(Car tour 6) or to Terchová. (see page 115). 30min on foot. Follow Walk 31 (page 128), commemorating Juraj Jánošík, to the 15min-point, for a picnic on the grass; retrace steps to Terchová.
Fine views across the small town of Terchová to the forested ranges of the Malá Fatra National Park.

Walking

The six national parks featured in this guide, in southernmost Poland and across Slovakia's mountain areas, offer an immense wealth of walks. There are easy to moderate outings through long valleys, and challenging, exhilarating ridge walks high above. Others take you to supremely beautiful tarns overlooked by rugged peaks, or into deep, seemingly impenetrable gorges. Many afford feasts of magnificent panoramic views across the ranges and surrounding valleys. Some include a visit to a mountain inn (*schronisko* or *chata*), usually accessible only on foot, where you can enjoy refreshments in the company of other walkers. Indeed, you'll rarely be alone for long anywhere, such is the popularity of walking with people of all ages in both countries. The walks all follow clearly defined paths and trails, many of which are tributes to the superlative skills of pathbuilders.

There are 31 main walks (and two alternatives), almost all of which have at least one shorter version. The 'Picnics and short walks' chapter includes 10 walks of between 45min and 1h30min in duration. They are also grouped by national park, where the walks are easily accessible from one or more bases. Whichever walks you choose, I hope they stimulate your enthusiasm, and that your visit is followed by several more to these beautiful, refreshingly unspoiled countries.

Grades, waymarks and maps

This guide offers a wide variety of walks with, I think, some to suit nearly all tastes and abilities. They are graded according to distance, amount of ascent, roughness of the terrain underfoot and specific challenges. **Easy walks** are suitable for anyone who is reasonably fit and active; **strenuous walks** will appeal to experienced hill walkers. Most of the walks cross some rocky terrain (almost unavoidable away from paved paths), and for some you need to be sure-footed and to have a head for heights. A few involve easy scrambling where it's necessary to use your hands to negotiate small, easily-angled rock outcrops. Although none of the walks require rock-climbing skills, some involve the use of **fixed chains and ladders**; in almost all such cases, alternatives are offered.

All the walks follow paths, trails or tracks which are **signposted and waymarked** with paint marks of various colours, usually flashes; the colours serve only to distinguish one route from another and are unrelated to difficulty or duration. For safety's sake, *it is essential to keep to these routes*, as **shown on the maps by an unbroken black line**.

The **maps** in this book are adequate for the walks described, but if you wish to venture further afield, you will need the relevant topographical map. Excellent, inexpensive topographical maps are very widely available in both countries. In Poland, the eye-catching Sygnatura/Polkart series (1:25,000 and 1:50,000) is recommended; for Slovakia, the VKÚ-Harmanec maps (1:25,000, 1:50,000) are first-rate. Other walks are shown in brochures available from tourist information and national park offices;

Equipment and safety

For all but Walk 3 (Dunajec Gorge), it is assumed that you would carry walking poles (if you use them). The contents of your pack must take account of the weather, time of the year, and duration of the walk.

- Always carry plenty of food and water.
- Wear walking boots with ankle support, except where indicated.
- Always carry extra clothing, including a waterproof jacket, even on warm days. Extra items are essential for mountain walks.
- Take sun protection cream, sunglasses and a shady hat.
- Carry a basic first aid kit.

Extra equipment for mountain walks
- Waterproof trousers
- Windproof jacket and fleece top
- Warm hat and gloves
- Water purifying tablets (or filter), if taking on water at streams
- Map, compass, whistle, mobile phone. The emergency number for mountain rescue in Poland is 0601 100 300 and in Slovakia 18 300. Mobile reception on mountain ridges and tops appears to be good in both countries, but unreliable on sheltered ground. The emergency numbers in Poland are 997 (police) and 999 (ambulance). In Slovakia call 112 to contact the integrated SOS system.

Safety
- Estimate your ability conservatively.
- Avoid walking alone; leave word of your intended route and check in when you return.
- Be aware of any escape routes and the time of the point of no return. Turn back if the route proves too difficult or if the weather deteriorates — thunderstorms can develop very quickly, especially in summer.
- Choose a low-level walk or plan a day's touring if storms are forecast.
- Remember that limestone rock (in the Pieniny, Slovenský Raj and Malá Fatra) becomes *very* slippery when wet.
- Take care on rocky paths across steep mountain slopes. Try to avoid knocking stones off the path; if this happens, shout a warning to anyone below.

Effects of altitude

Ten of the walks described in this guide reach a height exceeding 2000m, about 650m higher than Britain's highest summit, Ben Nevis. You may have heard of acute mountain sickness (AMS), brought about by lack of oxygen. Although normally this condition is likely to be experienced only above 2500m, we consider it important that you are aware of the symptoms and know the simple precautions to take.

AMS ('acute' meaning sudden-onset) happens because the lungs and heart must work harder to supply the body with oxygen. Symptoms are dizziness, headache, nausea and loss of appetite. However it's almost certain that the only effects you may notice are the need to exert a little more effort during the ascent and, perhaps, slight breathlessness. Experience indicates that age, gender and fitness are virtually irrelevant in determining potential sufferers. It is important to have plenty to drink and to rest whenever necessary — *don't push on beyond your normal climbing comfort level.*

Nevertheless, as you will spend only a short time at these exalted heights, the likelihood of experiencing AMS to any degree at all is *very* remote on any of the walks in this guide.

Weather

The area covered by this guide experiences a continental climate, with warm summers and cold winters. July and August are the warmest months but, together with June, among the wettest — and also the time when thunderstorms occur, usually during the afternoon. Apart from the winter months (November-March), autumn (September and October), is the driest time. Snow is likely at any time in the highest regions, and a certainty above 1000m from November to April. May is generally regarded as the start of spring, although the weather can be very unstable; the two autumn months, however, are usually the most stable time of the year. In Poland especially, most years are blessed with the 'golden Polish spring' from mid-September to the end of October: long spells of clear, calm sunny weather, when the autumn colours in the forests and woodlands are incredibly varied and beautiful. Prevailing winds are generally from the west.

The Polish Institute of Meteorology and Water Management issues daily on-line regional forecasts; part of the site is in English: www.imgw.pl. The Slovak equivalent, the Slovak Hydrometeorological Institute site (www.shmu.sk) does not, unfortunately, have an English version, although their forecasts are more clearly detailed, and include information for the 'Vysoké Tatry' (High Tatras).

The **best times** to visit the two areas in **Poland** are from **early May** for the Pieniny mountains and from **late May** in the Tatras **to the end of June**, and during **September** and **October**. In **Slovakia**, the season usually begins in Malá Fatra, Low Tatras and Slovenský Raj in **early May**; in the High Tatras the walking season begins on **15 June** (mountain paths are closed from 1 November until then). In all four areas, **autumn** (September and October) is probably the best time for a visit. July and August are universally busy, queues form along the most popular walking routes, and accommodation is at a premium.

Where to stay

All the walks start from a town or village with a choice of accommodation listed under 'Nearest accommodation', with an alternative location in some cases. Sources of information about accommodation are given below under 'Useful contacts'. If you prefer not to make reservations, local official tourist information offices are a reliable source of assistance, although this approach would be inadvisable during the July-August peak season. Accommodation in **private homes**, usually on a room-only basis, is plentifully available, except in the Low Tatras. Basic **campsites** for tourers and tents are few, but there is one near each of the featured national parks; most sites also have chalets for hire. The only **youth hostel** is that in Zakopane, the base for the Polish Tatras.

Nuisances

Although a few species of **snakes** live in Poland and Slovakia, I have only seen one solitary specimen during my walking trips in both countries, often in warm weather — so they can't really be regarded as nuisances.

You may encounter persistent and quite aggressive **beggars**, mostly children, in some areas near Slovenský Raj National Park. Pay no attention to them whatsoever and walk quickly away. Advice about one particular area to avoid at all costs, based on first-hand experience, is given with the relevant walk (see Walk 20, page 100).

Country code

Please keep all the following points in mind as you walk.

- Keep to waymarked paths and trails.
- Heed warning and advisory signs.
- Do not pick plants (including mushrooms), or disturb birds and animals.
- Do not damage signs or visitors' books.

- Avoid causing rock falls.
- Leave gates as you find them.
- Do not take dogs into national parks.
- Do not light fires or drop cigarettes or lighted matches.
- Take ***all*** your litter home — carry a plastic bag to do so.
- Greet local people with 'Dzień Dobry' (Poland) 'Dobrý deň' (Slovakia); for walkers 'Dobry/Grüss Gott/Hello' will almost always be reciprocated.

Polish for walkers

Polish, a Slavonic language, is a daunting challenge for English speakers. Fortunately it is phonetic so that, with a little practice, the clusters of consonants, the scarcity of vowels, and the presence of accents, become less intimidating. The use of a few basic phrases and words is always appreciated by local people. Hotel and tourist office staff generally do have some English, but otherwise it isn't widely spoken *as yet*, although this will probably change rapidly with growing tourism from Britain. In the meantime, German is quite widely understood. Below is a simple guide to pronunciation and some basic words and phrases you may find helpful.

pronunciation of vowels

a	as in cut
e	as in pet
i	as in pig
o	as in hot
u	as in cook
y	as in yard
ą	as on or om
ę	as en, or em, or e
o	same as Polish 'u'
ie	pronounced y-e
eu	pronounced e-u
ia	similar to 'yah'

pronunciation of consonants

ć, ch	as in per<u>ch</u>
cz	between the ch in church and the j in judge
dz	as in a<u>dds</u>
dź, dż	as d-sh, d-ch
g	as in guide
h	as in the Scottish lo<u>ch</u>
ł	as in <u>w</u>eek
ń, ni	as in o<u>ni</u>on
r	always trilled
rz	as zh or sh
ś	as in <u>sh</u>eep
szcz	as in fre<u>sh ch</u>eese
sz	as in <u>sh</u>oe
w	as in <u>v</u>alley

A few useful words and phrases

Hello	Dzień dobry
Good morning	Dobry rano
Good evening	Dobry wieczór
Goodbye	Do widzenia
Please	Proszę
Thank you	Dziekuję
Yes. No	Tak/Nie
You're welcome	Proszę
Do you speak English?	Czy pan/pani (m/f) mówi po angielsku?

I understand/don't understand	Rozumiem/nie rozumiem
Please write it down	Proszę to napisać
Where is?	Gdzie jest?
How far is it to?	Jak daleko jest do?
I'm lost	Zgubiłem/łam (m/f) sie
Help!	Ratunku!
straight ahead	prosto
left/right	lewo/prawo
near/far	blisko/daleko
early/late	wcześnie/poznie
easy/difficult	łatwy/trudny
small/large	mały/wielki
open/closed	otwarty, czynne/zamknięte
north/east/south/west	północ/wschód/południe/zachód
toilets	toalety
restaurant	restauracja/kawiarnia
bakery	piekarnia
hotel/guest house	hotel/pensjonat
hostel/camping	schronisko/kemping
drinking water	woda

Here are some other useful words, including those found on maps and in the text.

Polish	*English*
biuro	office
brama	gate
cmentarz	cemetery
deszcz	rain
dolina	valley
dom	house
drabinki	ladders
droga	road
góra	mountain
górka	hill
gran	ridge
granica	border
grzmot	thunderstorm
herbaciarnia	tearoom
jama, jaskinia	cave
jezioro	lake (large)
kaplica	chapel
klasztor	monastery
kolej linowo	cable car
kolej linowo terenowa	funicular
kolej krzesełkowa	chair lift
kósciół	church
lańcucky	chains

English	*Polish*
border	granica
bridge	most
cable car	kolejka linowa
castle	zamek
cave	jama, jaskinia
cemetery	cmentarz
chains	lańcucky
chair lift	kolej krzesełkowa
chapel	kaplica
church	kósciół
cliff	skała
field	pole
forest	las
funicular	kolej linowo terenowo
gate	brama
gorge, gully	zlab
guide	przewodnik
hiking/walking	wycieczki piesze
hill	górka
house	dom
island	wyspa
ladders	drabinki
lake (large)	jezioro
lake (small)	staw
map	mapa

Polish	*English*
las	forest
mapa	map
masyw	massif
miasto	town
most	bridge
perć	narrow path
polana	meadow
pole	field
potok	stream
przełęcz	pass, saddle
przewodnik	guide
punkt widikow	viewpoint
rynek	square
rzeka	river
schronisko	refuge
skała	cliff
sklep	shop
słońce	sun
staw	lake (small)
szczyt	summit
szieźką, szlak	path
ulica	street
wiata	picnic shelter
wiatr	wind
wierch	mountain
wies	village
wodospad	waterfall
wycieczki piesze	hiking
wyspa	island
zamek	castle
zlab	gorge
znakowany	waymarked
źródło	spring

English	*Polish*
massif	masyw
meadow	polana
monastery	klasztor
mountain	góra, wierch
mountain refuge	schronisko
office	biuro
pass, saddle	przełęcz
path	szieźką, szlak
path (narrow)	perć
peak	góra, wierch
picnic shelter	wiata
rain	deszcz
ridge	gran
river	rzeka
road	droga
shop	sklep
spring	źródło
square	rynek
stream	potok
street	ulica
summit	szczyt
sun	słońce
tearoom	herbaciarnia
thunderstorm	grzmot
town	miasto
valley	dolina
viewpoint	punkt widikow
village	wies
waterfall	wodospad
waymarked	znakowany
wind	wiatr

Slovak for walkers

Slovak is also a Slavonic language and only a little less difficult to tackle than Polish. It, too, is phonetic and has fewer awkward combinations of consonants — and one less accent! As always, learn a few basic phrases and words to pave the way with local people. Staff in hotels and most tourist offices speak at least some English, otherwise it's little known, except among young people. Again, this situation most likely will change with increasing tourism from Britain and other nationalities whose second language is English but, in the meantime, German is widely understood. A simple guide to pronunciation and some basic words and phrases for walking and touring follows.

pronunciation of vowels

a	as in cup
ä	as in mat
á	as in rather
e	as in fed
é	as in bear
i	as in machine
í	as in meet
ia	as in machine and cup
ie	as in machine and fed
iu	as in machine and look
o	as in hot
ó	as in shore
ô	as in swan
u	as in look
ú	as in choose
y	as in sit
ý	as in feet

pronunciation of consonants

c	as in lots
č	as in china
ch	as in Scottish loch
ď	as in dew
dz	as in roads
dž	as in jam
d', t', ň, l'	followed by a y sound, as in during, tutor, new, million
h	more forcefully than hand
j	as in yes
r	trilled
š	as in shoe

A few useful phrases and words

Hello	Dobrý deň
Good morning	Dobré ráno
Good evening	Dobrý večer
Goodbye	Do videnia
Please	Prosím
Thank you	Ďakujem
Yes. No	Áno. Nie
You're welcome	Prosím
Do you speak English?	Hovoríte anglicky?
I understand/don't understand	Rozumiem/Nerozumiem
Please write it down	Mohli by ste mi to napísat', prosím?
Help!	Pomoc!
I'm lost	Nevyznám sa tu
Where is..?	Kde je ...?
How far is it?	Jak je to d'aleko?
straight ahead	rovno
left/right	vl'avo/vpravo
near/far	blízko/d'aleko
early/late	skoro/neskoro
easy/difficult	l'ahké/t'ažké
little/big	vel'ký/malý
open/closed	otvorené/zatvorené
north/east/south/west	sever/východ/juh/západ
old/new	staré/nové
upper/lower	dolné/horné
toilets	záchody/WC/toalety
restaurant	reštaurácia/konoba/kavárieň
grocery/food shop	potraviny
hotel/guest house	hotel/penziónat
hostel/camping	turistická ubytovňa/ autokemping
drinking water	voda

Here are some other useful words, including those found on maps and in the text. *Note:* Words for some colours are included in this Slovak glossary because they often appear on path signposts indicating intersections.

Slovak	*English*
belasá	blue
burka	thunderstorm
červená	red
cesta	road
chata	mountain refuge
chodník	path
cierna	black
cintorín	cemetery
dážd'	rain
dolina	valley
dom	house
hora	mountain
hrad	castle
hranica	border
hrebeň	ridge
jaskyňa	cave
jazero	lake
kameň	rock
kapinka	chapel
kláštor	monastery
kostol	church
kotol/ kotline	shallow valley
lanovka	funicular
les	forest
mapa	map
mesto	town
most	bridge
námestie	square
pešia túra	hiking/ walking
planina	valley basin
pleso	tarn
pol'ana	field
potok	stream
prameň	spring
prehliadka	lookout
rázcestie	junction
rebrika	ladder
ret'az	chain
rieka	river
sedačkova lanovka	chair lift
sedlo	pass
skala	crag
slnečno	sunny
štít	peak

English	*Slovak*
black	čierna
blue	belasá
border	hranica
bridge	most
castle	hrad
cave	jaskyňa
cemetery	cintorín
chain	ret'az
chair lift	sedačkova lanovka
chapel	kapinka
church	kostol
crag	skala
field	pol'ana
forest	les
funicular	lanovka
gorge/gully	žl'ab
green	zelená
hiking/walking	pešia túra
hill	vrch
house	dom
junction	rázcestie
ladder	rebrika
lake	jazero
lookout	prehliadka
map	mapa
monastery	kláštor
mountain	hora
mountain refuge	chata
pass	sedlo
peak	štít
path	chodník
picnic shelter	turistika prístrešok
precipice	zráz
rain	dážd'
red	červená
ridge	hrebeň
river	rieka
road	cesta
rock	kameň
spring	prameň
square	námestie
stream	potok
street	ulica
summit	vrchol

Slovak	*English*
turistika prístrešok	picnic shelter
ulica	street
vietor	wind
vodopád	waterfall
vrch	hill
vrchol	summit
vyhliadka	viewpoint
zelená	green
žľab	gorge/gully
žltá	yellow
značený	waymarked
zráz	precipice

English	*Slovak*
sunny	slnečno
tarn	pleso
thunderstorm	burka
town	mesto
valley	dolina
valley (shallow)	kotol/ kotline
valley basin	planina
viewpoint	vyhliadka
waterfall	vodopád
waymarked	značený
wind	vietor
yellow	žltá

Organisation of the walks

The walks are grouped according to the car tour from which they are accessible, and by national parks and individual bases within those areas. The tours comprise a clockwise circuit from the Pieniny Mountains in Poland to the Malá Fatra National Park in central western Slovakia, as can be seen on the fold-out touring map. The walks are circular, linear or out-and-back.

Signposting on Walk 27

At the top of each walk you will find essential information: distance and ***walking time (without stops)***, grade, equipment, availability of refreshments, transport, nearest accommodation and — in almost all cases — alternative shorter walks. *Do check your walking times against mine on a short walk before venturing on a longer hike.*

Below is a key to the symbols on the walking maps.

motorway	spring, waterfall	bus stop
main road	difficult path	car parking
secondary road	hotel.restaurant	funicular railway
town or minor road	café or bar	cable car or ski lift
motorable track/lane	mountain inn	castle, fort
waymarked route	campsite	cave
path, trail, track	monastery.church	specified building
2→ main walk	chapel.cross, shrine	monument
2→ alternative walk	cemetery	transmitter, mast
400 height in metres	picnic tables.shelter	*P* picnic suggestion
	best views	map continuation

POLAND'S PIENINY NATIONAL PARK

Pieniny National Park (Pieniński Park Narodowy; Walks 1-3) protects part of the Pieniny Mountains on the Slovak border, about 30km northeast of the Tatra Mountains. A small, compact park (2346ha/5797acres), it was set aside in the early 1930s. Its spectacular limestone peaks, spires and pinnacles are surrounded by forests of beech, sycamore, alder and pine, interspersed with beautiful meadows. The spectacular river Dunajec extends for 7km along the eastern boundary and forms part of the border with Slovakia and its Pieninský Národný Park.

The highest summit in the Polish park is Okraglica (982m), one of the Trzy Korony (Three Crowns), a very popular destination with Polish walkers. Some 35km of waymarked paths and trails bring many of the park's peaks, valleys and ridges within easy reach. The park has an exceptionally rich and varied flora (1100 species of plants) and is home to 95 species of birds and numerous mammals. A small entry fee is charged, usually collected at one of the more frequented path junctions within the park.

The park's website, www.pieninypn.pl, has an informative English language section.

The town of Nowy Targ is the transport centre for this park. It is on the Kraków/Zakopane railway line; Kraków/Zakopane buses operated by PKS and other companies stop here too (departures approximately every hour). Some services continue to Krościenko and Szczawnica, two small towns just outside the park to the north which provide amenable bases. PKS operates the service from Nowy Targ to Krościenko and Szczawnica with approximately five departures daily, and a few more Mon-Fri during peak season. See transport details for Walks 1-3 on page 133. It is also possible to reach Zakopane from Krościenko and Szczawnica without changing at Nowy Targ, though the service is limited outside the peak season (1/6-30/9).

Photograph: windswept pine in the Pieniny National Park

Walk 1 (Pieniny): THE THREE CROWNS

See also photograph on pages 46-47
Distance: 8km/5mi; 3h5min
Grade: moderate, with approximately 580m/1900ft ascent on waymarked and signposted minor road, tracks, trails and paths. The final ascent of Okraglica is via a very firmly secured metal bridge and steps, with handrails on both sides; the small summit, enclosed by a railing, drops very steeply on three sides and demands a head for heights.
Equipment: see page 31
Refreshments: available in Krościenko. There is one source of water along the way, at Pieński Potok (see map).
Transport: 🚗 (Car tour 1) or 🚌 (see page 40 and Transport, page 133) to Krościenko. Travelling by car, there is a small car park in Krościenko beside Ulica Trzech Koron (on the route of the walk; see walk description for directions), but it usually fills up quickly. Otherwise there's a large, pay car park in Krościenko: drive west along the main road from the river Dunajec bridge for 250m; turn left along a road (Ulica Mickiewicza) signposted 'Policja' to Ulica Rynek (the main square) and bear right to the nearby car park, on the left. All buses to Krościenko stop in Ulica Rynek, where the walk begins.
Nearest accommodation: Krościenko, Szczawnica

The Trzy Korony (Three Crowns) are the outstanding landmark of Pieniny National Park and a very popular destination with Polish walkers of all ages. Many seem happy simply to walk there and back along the same path, but the slightly longer loop route described here takes in the remains of an unusual 13th-century castle. The beech and sycamore forests are magnificent, especially during autumn, while the tranquillity of the meadows scattered across the steep mountain slopes contrasts beautifully with the dramatic ruggedness of the limestone cliffs above.

Start the walk in **Krościenko**, on the southwestern corner of Ulica Rynek, outside a bank. A discreet cluster of signs here includes three pointing west to green- and yellow-waymarked routes; follow them along Ulica Mickiewicza to the main road (Ulica Jagiellońska) and turn left. After approximately 250m turn left up a cobbled minor road, Ulica Trzech Koron. This rises steeply up past a 'Pienińśki Park Narodowy' **notice board** and signposts; then, within about 100m, you pass a small parking

Two-lane metal steps on the approach to Okraglica, the highest of the Trzy Korony

area on the right (if it's not full, motorists could park here).

The cobbles end at the last house, from where you follow a track steeply up through trees. When you reach a wide meadow, the fine view of Krościenko shown on pages 46-47 soon provides a good reason to pause. From a notice board at a trail junction on the **national park boundary** (**32min**), continue straight on, following blue and yellow waymarks. The trail soon bends right across a meadow and into deciduous forest, climbing steeply. Bear left at a fork and go on, past a junction on the left called **Banków Groník** (**41min**), again along a trail. **Pieński Potok** (**49min**), a stream, has been partly diverted along a hollowed-out log for easy filling of water bottles.

There's more climbing before you reach the next junction, where you turn left towards *Zamkowa Góra* (Castle Mountain), following blue waymarks (**54min**). The trail undulates through forest — the

beeches are huge — and becomes a stepped path that leads around a small valley to a long flight of steps up to **Zamkowa Góra (1h16min)**, the highest castle in Poland. Above you is a sizeable fragment of the castle and to the right is a **shrine**; unfortunately the information board is in Polish only. Climb another flight of steps to a lookout platform beside a more extensive section of the superbly built castle wall.

From the information board, continue up more steps, then go along a short log-supported path with a firm handrail beside a high cliff. Numerous steps carry you steeply up — through, between and across limestone outcrops — to the **crest of the ridge**. But you're only there for a moment. You then go down to a path junction called **Polana Kosarzyska (1h24min)**, where you keep straight ahead.

Press on, up the meadow and into the forest, with little respite, to a trail point called **Niedźwiadki (1h35min)** and up onto the crest,

Forest trail near Niedźwiadki

from where it's not far to the **Trzy Korony (1h38min)**. If this seems an anti-climax, with the tiers of picnic benches and the national park fee collector's tiny shelter, well, you're not quite there yet. (There's a much quieter picnic area a short distance along the signposted path towards *Przełęcz Szopka.*)

The summit of **Okraglica**, the highest of the Trzy Korony, is at the end of two metal bridges (with up and down lanes), and a flight of steps. The platform is often crowded, with good reason. The panoramic view is exceptionally varied — the river Dunajec directly below, the striped patchwork of fields beyond, the nearby rugged grey-white spires, and the High Tatras on the skyline to the west.

Back at the Trzy Korony path junction (**1h48min**), set off down a trail towards *Przełęcz Szopka,* following blue waymarks. You cross a meadow, pass a **picnic shelter (1h51min)** and descend steeply to a junction at the saddle, **Przełęcz Szopka (2h6min)**. Continue on the yellow trail towards *Krościenko,* through a succession of beautiful meadows, back to the Zamkowa Góra junction (**2h14min**). From here retrace your steps to **Banków Groñik (2h22min)**, the **national park boundary (2h35min)**, then go steeply downhill to the main road (**2h55min**) and turn right, back to **Krościenko (3h5min)**.

Walk 2 (Pieniny): THE SOKOLICA RIDGE

See map on pages 42-43
Distance: 10km/6.2mi; 3h53min
Grade: moderate, with approximately 650m/2130ft ascent, on signposted and waymarked minor road, track, trails and paths
Equipment: see page 31
Refreshments: available in Szczawnica, Ląd (near the bridge over the Grajcarek), Krościenko; spring at nearby Pieński Potok
Transport: (Car tour 1) or (see page 40 and Transport, page 133) to Szczawnica. Return on from Krościenko — back to Szczawnica for your car, or back to base. Motorists can park in Szczawnica near the Palenica chair lift station: turn off the main road opposite a leafy park, following signposting to *Kolej Línowa Palenica*. Alternatively, you can park near the hamlet of Ląd and join the walk at the 23min-point. Driving from Krościenko, turn right off the Krościenko/Szczawnica road 3km southeast of Krościenko, signposted *Parking*. Driving from Szczawnica, turn left off the Szczawnica/Krościenko road 1.7km southwest of Szczawnica, following a sign, *'P 500m'*, then turn right at a junction. This large parking area, on the north side of the river Grajcarek bridge at its confluence with the river Dunajec, offered free parking at time of writing. From this car park, walk across the bridge (closed to motor vehicles) to join the walk.
Nearest accommodation: Szczawnica, Krościenko

Shorter walk: **Czertezik summit from Krościenko**. 7.3km/4.4mi; 2h25min. Easy-moderate, with approximately 360m/1082ft ascent. Equipment: see page 31. Refreshments available only at Krościenko. Transport: or to/from Krościenko (see Walk 1, page 41). **Start out** at Ulica Rynek, the main square in **Krościenko** (where the buses stop). From the walkers' signposts on the southwestern corner of the square (outside a bank), follow Ulica Mickiewicza to the main road and turn left for about 250m, to a cobbled minor road, Ulica Trzech Koron. Turn left and walk steeply up, past a national park **notice board**, then a small **car park** on the right. Beyond the last house a track leads on steeply through trees. At a path junction (**32min**) bear left along the green-waymarked trail; it rises steadily, soon past a good view of Krościenko, then mostly through forest to a junction called **Burzana** (**49min**). Continue for about 100m to an unsignposted junction and bear left along a path traversing the steep slope. You rise to another junction, this one called **Czertezik** (**54min**). The peak itself is above you here, so turn right up to the summit of **Czertezik** (**56min**) — well worth the short ascent. You have now joined the main walk at the 2h19min-point: follow it back to **Krościenko** (**2h25min**).

A comparatively long and intermittently rocky ridge rising steeply southwards from the river Dunajec and overlooking the small town of Krościenko provides the setting for this extremely scenic day's outing. The views of the river's deep gorge and of the Trzy Korony (Walk 1) are superb and, although the route is popular, it doesn't seem to attract quite as many walkers as does the Trzy Korony route.

The Shorter walk, a circuit from Krościenko, visits all but one of the peaks along the ridge.The main, linear walk, takes advantage of a small punt which takes you across the river Dunajec, to the point where you start the climb to the ridge. The punt operates on demand from mid-April to the end of October, from 8am until at least 5pm. It runs from a jetty just over 1km south of the Grajcarek bridge; the fare is nominal.

Begin the walk in **Szczawnica**: cross the **Palenica chair lift** car park and skirt the hotel to reach the footbridge across the **river Grajcarek** (at time of writing the chair lift was being upgraded; normally, access to the bridge may be more direct). On the far side of the bridge, a stone-paved path, then a minor road lead you downstream to the hamlet of **Łąd**, near the confluence of the rivers Grajcarek and Dunajec (**23min**). A road comes in from the right here — from the large, optional parking area mentioned under 'Transport' above. Follow the minor road, Droga Pienińska, upstream, past a national park **information centre** (supposedly open daily) to a **jetty** (**36min**) below the boatman's small roadside shed. From here you take the **punt across the river Dunajec**.

Once on the far side of the river, turn left along a short path to the signposted start of the route to *Sokolica*. The trail climbs fairly steeply at first, past a meadow with a good view of part of Szczawnica (**45min**; Picnic 1). Flights of wooden steps ease the ascent of the steepish slope. From another meadow (**56min**) more steps wind up a well-designed route to a signposted junction (**1h10min**).

Now climb the steep steps, with a helpful handrail, to the rocky summit of **Sokolica** (**1h16min**) directly above the river Dunajec. Trzy Korony's cliffs dominate the view to the west, and the High

Tatras may be visible beyond on a clear day; in autumn the palette of colours on the forested slopes is truly beautiful.

Return to the signposted junction (**1h37min**) and descend to a saddle called **Przełęcz Sosnow**. Then go up via natural and man-made rock steps to the narrow crest, from where more steps lead on to summit of **Czertezik (2h19min)**, with spectacular gorge and mountain vistas. *(The Shorter walk joins here).*

From the summit descend to a path junction, confusingly called **Czertezik (2h20min)**. Here you have a choice for the next section of the walk: the more adventurous blue-waymarked route signposted towards *Zamkowa Góra* or the easier, green-waymarked route to the right. *The following times assume you've followed the blue route.*

For the blue route, climb rock steps (with a handrail) to a short stretch along the narrow ridge, then climb rock and log-supported steps to the summit of **Czerteż** for an even better view of the Trzy Korony. Descend via rock steps to a trail which leads to an unsignposted junction with the green route, and continue to the nearby intersection at a junction called **Burzana (2h32min)**.

For the green route, simply follow the path down and across the steep slope, then up to an unsignposted junction, to rejoin the blue route and to go on to a junction called **Burzana** (reached in six minutes).

Both routes continue from Burzana: climb easy steps to a short ridge-top path, then descend through a meadow (**2h52min**). Then rise up again, to another peak, **Sutrówka**, from where there is a fine view of the almost vertical cliffs below the summit of Sokolica. The trail then dips, rises once more to the broad ridge and quite promptly descends to a junction called **Banków Groñik (3h10min)**.

Continue down to the **national park boundary (3h23min)**, walk on to the main road (**3h43min**) and turn right into **Krościenko (3h53min)**. Buses back to Szczawnica leave from Ulica Rynek, the main square.

View down over Krościenko from the lower reaches of Walks 1 and 2

Walk 3 (Pieniny): DUNAJEC GORGE

See map on pages 42-43
Distance: 23.6km/14.6mi; 5h40min
Grade: easy-moderate, with negligible ascent, on minor roads, unsurfaced roads and paved paths
Equipment: see page 31; walking shoes or sandals are suitable. ***Carry your passport or ID card*** for the border crossings.
Refreshments: available in Szczawnica, at Łąd (near the bridge over the river Grajcarek) and possibly near Červený Kláštor
Transport: 🚗 (Car tour 1) or 🚌 (see page 40 and Transport, page 133) to Szczawnica. Travelling by car, see Walk 2, page 45, for parking advice in Szczawnica or near the hamlet of Łąd. In the latter case, join the main walk at the 23min-point.
Nearest accommodation: Szczawnica, Krościenko
Shorter walks
1 Pol'anka. 14km/8.7mi; 2h48min. Easy, with negligible ascent. Equipment and transport as for the main walk. Follow the main walk to the 1h24min-point and retrace steps from there.
2 Huta. 18.6km/11.5mi; 4h8min. Easy, with negligible ascent. Equipment and transport as for main walk. Follow the main walk to the 2h4min-point and retrace steps from there.

The spectacular 7km-long gorge of the river Dunajec is traditionally traversed by raft from the village of Sromowce Kąty to a point near Szczawnica. However, it's also possible to walk right through the gorge on an unsurfaced road, enjoying the magnificent scenery at leisure. Another advantage of being on foot is that you see the gorge from both directions, as there's no choice but to retrace your steps. On a fine day, numerous rafts should float past; the gorge is also a magnet for the more adventurous canoeists.

You will cross the Poland-Slovakia border in the course of the walk; the passport control check point is open from 9am-9pm (April-Sept) and 9am-5pm (Oct-Mar). In Slovakia you walk through the Pieninský National Park, where some interesting information boards about the park (with English text) are spaced along the road. Unfortunately, the Slovak hamlet of Červený Kláštor, almost 1km beyond the end of the gorge, is rather a disappointment: just a campsite, a bar-restaurant and a dour monastery — scarcely worth the extra distance, so you may wish to turn back at the 2h36min-point.

Begin the walk in **Szczawnica**: cross the **Palenica chair lift** car park and skirt the hotel to reach the footbridge across the **river Grajcarek** (at time of writing the chair lift was being upgraded; normally, access to the bridge may be more direct). On the far side of the bridge, a stone-paved path, then a minor road lead you downstream to the hamlet of **Łąd**, near the confluence of the rivers Grajcarek and Dunajec (**23min**). A road comes in from the right here — from the large, optional parking area mentioned under 'Transport' above. Follow the minor road, Droga Pienińska, upstream, past a national park **information centre** (supposedly open daily), then a small roadside shed near a jetty used by the boatman ferrying walkers to the Sokolica path (Walk 2; **36min**).

Rafting on the Dunajec

Keep ahead here, to enter the **Dunajec Gorge**: walk on through the **border crossing (43min)** and, about 50m further on, at a broad U-bend in the river, bear left along the signposted *'Hiking Path'*. At a junction with the road to the village of Lesnica (**49min**), below an immense wall of grey-white limestone, go straight ahead and continue along the unsurfaced road beyond the barrier (Picnic 2; picnic shelter).

Further on, the huge wedge of limestone that forms Sokolica's summit comes into view (**1h**). Beyond a broad bend, you come to **Pol'anka (1h24min)**, once the site of an inn, now a sheltered glade beside the road, with a picnic table. *(Shorter walk 1 returns from here).*

The river changes character constantly: surging rapids, shoals, quiet pools, tiny islands, with the towering cliffs, pinnacles and spires above. Around a sharp bend, past steep cliffs, you soon reach a track junction called **Huta** (**2h4min**). *(Shorter walk 2 returns from here.)*

Beyond Huta the river flows through a quieter stretch, then you come to the impressive cliffs at the entrance to the gorge, and the road swings away from the river (**2h36min**; picnic tables). Soon tarmac comes under foot. Further on, you can turn right opposite the office of the adjacent **camping ground**, to cross a footbridge, and 50m further on you may find that a small bar-restaurant is open, in the shadow of the monastery, **Červený Kláštor (2h50min)**.

Retrace your steps to return. On the way back, you soon appreciate the different perspective at the gorge entrance, with the dramatic prospect of two enormous isolated blades of rock. Approximate timings for landmarks on the return are: **Huta (3h36min)**, the **border crossing (4h57min)** and the junction at **Ląd (5h17min)**, where the road to the left leads to a car parking area. Eventually you are back at the starting point, the **Palenica chair lift** car park at **Szczawnica (5h40min)**.

POLAND'S TATRA NATIONAL PARK

Poland's Tatra National Park (Tatrzanski Park Narodowy; Walks 4-10) occupies 21,000ha/52,000 acres of the High Tatra Mountains, slightly more than a quarter of the entire range. Consisting mainly of heavily glaciated granite, the park is bounded on three sides by the border with Slovakia and its Tatranský Národný Park and in the north by the foothills rising from the valley of the youthful Dunajec River.

The highest peak is Rysy (2499m) above Morskie Oko (see Walk 10); several others exceed 2000m. Long, deep and readily accessible valleys extend from the Dunajec Valley south and southwestwards far up into the mountains; in the east, they are characterised by clusters of tarns in the uppermost reaches. Among four distinct vegetation zones, the most extensive are the forests of spruce, mountain ash and white birch, and outcrops of hardy dwarf pine. The park was established in 1954 and, together with its Slovak counterpart, was declared a Unesco Biosphere Reserve in 1992.

High up in each of the main valleys you'll find a mountain refuge or inn *(schronisko)*. Most reflect local architectural traditions and have been built since the late 1940s; they provide refreshments during the day and simple overnight accommodation. Hundreds of kilometres of waymarked paths throughout the park traverse the valleys and ridges and reach many of the summits. A small daily fee is charged, paid at one of the park entrances.

Zakopane, the lively town at the foot of the mountains and a colourful blend of traditional wooden buildings and modern edifices, is the natural base for exploring the park. It is at the end of the train line from Kraków, with at least four departures daily; duration of the rather tortuous journey varies widely from 3h45min to 5h. PKS and other bus companies provide a daily, more frequent (approximately hourly) and faster service. There is also a twice-daily PKS bus service between Zakopane and Poprad (Slovakia); the PKS service to Łysa Polana provides more frequent departures, to link with Slovak SAD buses across the border at Łysa Polana. There is also a mainly seasonal service between Zakopane and the Pieniny National Park towns, bases for Walks 1-3 (see page 40). See transport details for Walks 4-10 on page 133.

Photograph: Prezdni Staw and Wielki Staw (Walk 10)

Walk 4 (Polish High Tatras): DOLINA BIAŁEGO AND STRĄŻYSKA DOLINA VIA SARNIA SKAŁA

Distance: 10.1km/6.1mi; 3h40min
Grade: easy-moderate (550m/1800ft ascent); on signposted and waymarked paths and trails
Equipment: see page 31
Refreshments: available at the entrance to Dolina Białego (where there are also portable toilets), at Herbaciarnia Palenica (a tearoom in upper Strążyska Dolina) and at the entrance to Strążyska Dolina
Transport: 🚗 (Car tours 1 and 7), 🚆 or 🚌 to Zakopane (see page 50). Travelling by car, from Zakopane follow Ulica Kościeliska, Ulica Kasprusie and Ulica Strążyska to the entrance to Strążyska Dolina, where there's a pay car park. Travelling by public transport, take the minibus from opposite Zakopane bus station to the Strążyska Dolina car park and back (see Transport, page 133).
Nearest accommodation: Zakopane
Shorter walk: **Strążyska Dolina.** 4.6km/2.8mi; 2h. Easy (174m/570ft ascent). Equipment as for the main walk; refreshments available at the entrance to Strążyska Dolina and at the Herbaciarnia Palenica. Transport as for the main walk. Simply follow the wide trail up the valley to Strążyska Polana where you'll find Herbaciarnia Palenica (a tearoom); join the main walk here and retrace your steps to the start.

This walks offers an easy introduction to the Polish Tatra Mountains and the national park: you rise up through a dramatically beautiful valley to a scenic viewpoint, then descend to a secluded tearoom below the towering cliffs of Giewont (see Walk 5), with an attractive waterfall nearby. The return is down another pleasant, wooded valley.

Start the walk from the **Strążyska Dolina car park**: walk towards the national park entrance gate, but shortly turn left along a path between railings. Cross a bridge and follow the broad trail, Droga pod Reglami, along the edge of the forest, with fine views to Zakopane across the meadows (Picnic 4). When you reach the **Dolina Białego** entrance to the national park (**14min**), turn right along a wide trail (yellow waymarks) leading into this valley, soon walking beside the tumbling stream, **Biały Potok**. Cliffs on

Biały Potok

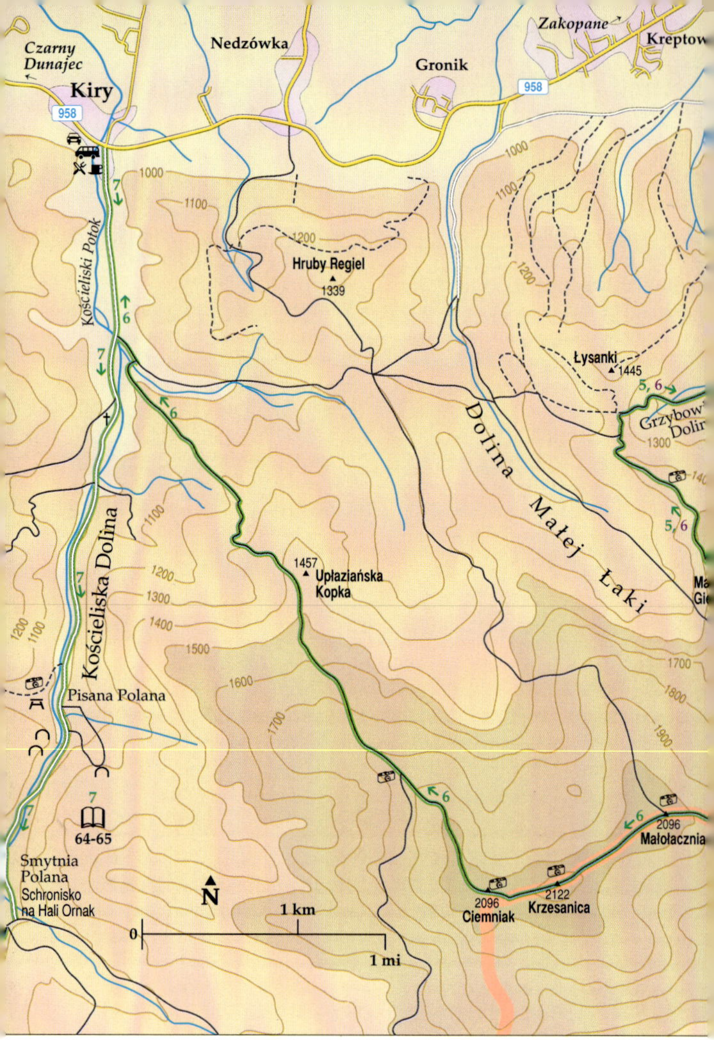

either side close in and you pass through a small gorge. Bridges cross the stream several times as you gain height past delightful pools and cascades.

From the uppermost bridge (**1h4min**) the path climbs away from the stream, steeply at first, then less so, to a junction with a black-waymarked route. Bear right here towards *Polana Strążyska* (**1h25min**). The path crosses an intermittently dry stream and rises quite steeply through a stand of mountain ash trees, their berries vivid red in September, to **Czerwona Przełęcz**, a grassy glade shaded by conifers (**1h45min**).

To reach the viewpoint on Sarnia Skała, follow the signposted path from here — steeply up, across another glade and on to the base of the crag. Bear right and climb the natural steps in the large boulders to the flat summit of **Sarnia Skała** (**1h56min**). The vista embraces the broad Zakopane valley and the Gubałówka ridge to the north; in the opposite

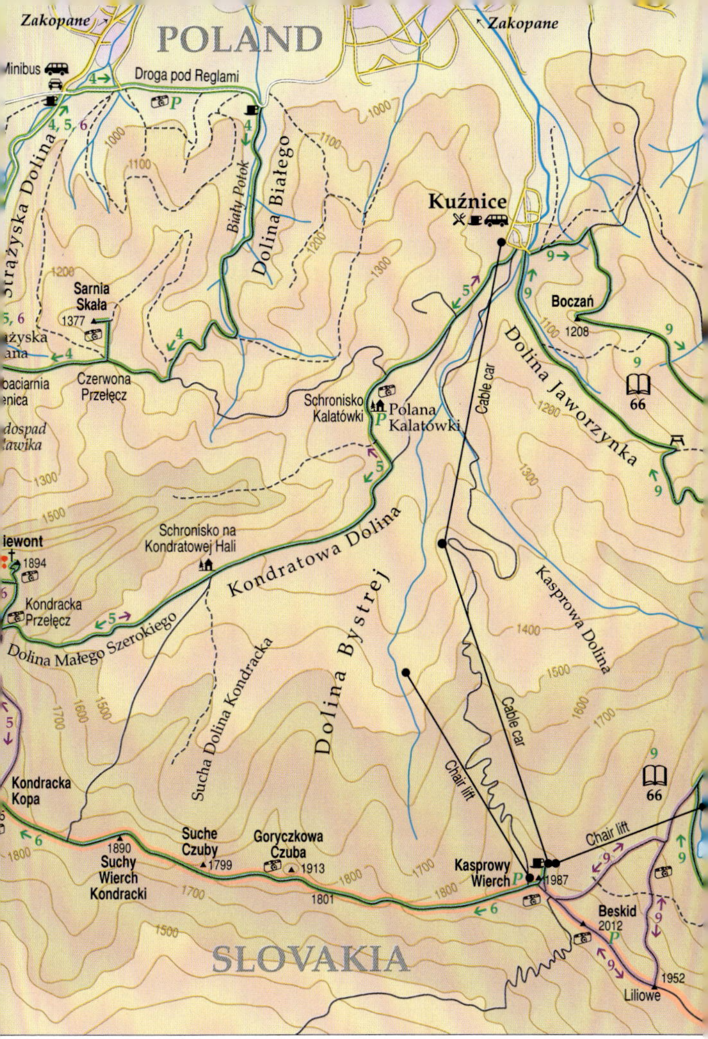

direction, Giewont (Walk 5) is readily identified by the large summit cross.

Return to the main path (**2h5min**) and continue to the right, steeply down to a path junction on the edge of a small meadow, **Strążyska Polana** (**2h28min**), where you'll find the **Herbaciarnia Palenica** tea room.

Turn left at the junction, soon crossing a log bridge, and go on along an easy path and over one more bridge to the waterfall, **Wodospad Siklawica** (**2h35min**); dramatically overlooked by Giewont's cliffs, it streams down a mossy rock wall into a small pool.

Back at the meadow (**2h41min**), you'll need your phrasebook to interpret Herbaciarnia Palenica's extensive menu of drinks, snacks and meals. *(The Shorter walk joins here.)*

The descent through the wooded valley, **Strążyska Dolina**, is straightforward. Follow the broad trail back downhill to the **car park** (**3h40min**).

Walk 5 (Polish High Tatras): THE ASCENT OF GIEWONT

See map on pages 52-53; see also cover photograph
Distance: 11.7km/7.3mi; 5h15min
Grade: moderate-strenuous (910m/2985ft ascent); on sign-posted and waymarked trails and paths. The final ascent to Giewont, and the start of the descent, have chain handrails and some stone steps; exposure is minimal and climbing skills are *not* required.
Equipment: see page 31
Refreshments: available at Kuźnice, Schronisko Kalatówki, Schronisko na Kondratowej Hali, Herbaciarnia Palenica and at the finish, Strążyska Dolina
Transport: 🚗 (Car tours 1 and 7), 🚆 or 🚌 to Zakopane (see page 50), then car or bus to Kuźnice. Those travelling by bus can either use a regular service or private minibus; return by private minibus (see Transport, page 133). Motorists: the car park nearest the walk (with very limited space) is 1km north of Kuźnice, at the roadside near the junction of Ulica P Tatrzańskich and Ulica M Karłowicza (see town plan)
Nearest accommodation: Zakopane

Shorter walk: **Schronisko na Kondratowej Hali.** 7km/4.3mi; 2h. Easy, with 308m/1010ft ascent. Equipment and transport as for the main walk. Refreshments available at Kuźnice and Schronisko Kalatówki. Follow the main walk to Schronisko na Kondratowej Hali (the 1h3min-point) and retrace steps from there.

Alternative walk: Kondracka Kopa. 13.9km/8.6mi; 5h39min. Strenuous, with 1080m/3540ft ascent. Equipment and transport as for main walk. Follow the main walk to the 1h58min-point. From the saddle, **Kondracka Przełęcz**, continue south on the yellow-waymarked route, steeply at first, then less so, up to the summit of **Kondracka Kopa** (**2h34min**), just on the border with Slovakia. There's so much in the panoramic view, that it's difficult to assimilate easily — the long Slovakian valleys, the jagged peaks to the east and the immense valley around Zakopane to the north. Return to **Kondracka Przełęcz** and rejoin the main walk (**3h6min**).

Giewont (1894m) is the most readily identifiable peak in the central Polish Tatras, topped by a very tall cross and standing apart from and to the north of the main range. The ascent is extremely popular, seemingly almost a duty for Polish walkers. Approached from the south, the final part of the climb is equipped with lengths of very securely placed chain handrails and some cut steps across steep crags. Special skills are *not* required and, although it helps to have a head for heights in a couple of places, you are *never* teetering over yawning depths! The popularity of this walk is unavoidably obvious in the surfaces of the rocks on the paths, burnished smooth by the passage of countless booted feet, and therefore potentially slippery. The views from the summit are due reward, taking in the main Tatras range and the Zakopane valley. If the prospect of using chains (see photograph opposite) is unappealing, Kondracka Kopa, a nearby peak on the ridge that forms the Polish/Slovak border, offers a straightforward although slightly longer ascent, and an equally good view: see the Alternative walk, and retrace your steps from Kondracka Kopa.

Start the walk in **Kuźnice**, about 50m east of the steps to the cable car station. Take the wide cobbled trail signposted to *Giewont* and waymarked in blue. Soon the trail forks; pay the modest national park fee here, then bear right along the wide shady trail, up past the junction with a yellow-waymarked route. Then bear right again at a fork, and pass another path junction on the right (**27min**). Shortly the trail levels out and leads into **Polana Kalatówki**, a meadow dominated by the large **Schronisko Kalatówki** (**30min**; Picnic 5). From here you can see the buildings at

Descending from Giewont

Schronisko na Kondratowej Hali

the top of the Kasprowy Wierch cable car route far above to the southeast. Bear left, up past the hotel, to meet a minor path near some picnic benches, and continue along a path towards the forest. Descend slightly to join another path and bear right, then right again, soon starting to gain height. The path undulates, to meet a trail which leads on to a meadow and another refuge, **Schronisko na Kondratowej Hali** (**1h3min**). *(The Shorter walk returns from here.)*

Follow the blue-waymarked route to the right; it soon bends right into a short valley, **Dolina Małego Szerokiego**, and rises sharply towards the saddle at its head. Water bottles can be filled at two streams (**1h36min**, **1h38min**). Well-designed zigzags take you up to the saddle, **Kondracka Przełęcz** (**1h58min**). *(This is where the Alternative walk diverts to Kondracka Kopa.)*

Turn northwards towards Giewont rising impressively ahead, along the beaten path. Rocky in places, it skirts a cluster of crags then crosses a minor saddle, just above which is a path junction at the foot of the Giewont massif (**2h11min**). From here the stepped path rises steeply to a short passage with a chain handrail, then another with steps cut into the cliffs, up to the summit of **Giewont** (**2h30min**). The western skyline is filled with peaks of multifarious profiles, while to the north Zakopane, its valley and the elongated Gubałówka ridge provide fascinating contrasts.

The descent is initially via a route separate from that of the ascent, down a chain-protected slope and then down steps in a steeply-angled crag. Descend these one step at a time, facing the cliff and holding the chain in both hands, until you reach a small flat area. A short easy scramble (again with a chain) follows, then you rejoin the uphill path and descend to the path junction (**2h55min**).

Continue west downhill on the red-waymarked route, to a small saddle. From here the path veers right to traverse below the cliffs of **Mały Giewont**, then rounds a bend and rises in steps up to a gap between a large boulder and the mountainside (**3h35min**). The traverse continues, generally down and into forest, then across a small clearing. A low knoll beside the path provides an excellent view of Giewont's cliffs (**4h**); three minutes further on there's a good viewpoint westwards a few steps to the left of the path.

The path leads back into forest and down to a junction (**4h10min**). Turn right, following both red and black waymarks, to descend **Grzybowiecka Dolina**, twice crossing a stream. Beyond a wide bridge, a trail leads you to **Strążyska Polana** and the undoubtedly welcome tea room, **Herbaciarnia Palenica** (**4h 48min**). The last part of the walk is straightforward: follow the trail down through the pleasantly wooded **Strążyska Dolina** to the **car park** (**5h15min**), where the minibuses wait.

Walk 6 (Polish High Tatras): ALONG THE POLAND-SLOVAKIA BORDER RIDGE

See map on pages 52-53
Distance: 12.4km/7.4mi; 5h43min
Grade: moderate (approximately 440m/1440ft ascent); on paths, trails and a sometimes-rough unsurfaced road
Equipment: see page 31
Refreshments: available at Kasprowy Wierch and Kiry
Transport: see Walk 5, page 54; then 🚡 from Kuźnice to Kasprowy Wierch (the fare includes the national park entry fee). Return on 🚌 from Kiry to Zakopane (see Transport, page 133).
Nearest accommodation: Zakopane
Shorter walk: Kondracka Kopa. 11km/6.8mi; 5h22min. Easy-moderate (approximately 310m/1020ft ascent). Equipment and transport as for the main walk, but return by minibus from Strążyska Dolina (same return transport as Walk 5). Refreshments are available at Kasprowy Wierch, Herbaciarnia Palenica at the head of Strążyska Dolina, and at the end of the walk. Follow the main walk to the 2h2min-point. Descend via the yellow-waymarked route to a path junction at **Kondracka Przełęcz** and continue, now with blue waymarks, to the junction near the **base of Giewont** (**3h2min**). Continue down on the red-waymarked route by following the notes for Walk 5 from the 2h55min-point (page 56) to **Herbaciarnia Palenica** (a tearoom; **4h55min**). Continue down the valley, **Strążyska Dolina,** to the end of the road and waiting minibuses (**5h22min**).

The high ridge forming part of the Poland-Slovakia border provides outstandingly scenic walking, in places demanding climbing skills and a good head for heights. Fortunately there is a lengthy section without any such challenges, quite narrow in places certainly, but not exposed. The cable car from Kuźnice to Kasprowy Wierch provides an effortless ascent, saving about 800m of climbing. There's little to recommend the alternative (which takes about 2h15min) — a waymarked path that seems to climb forever and saps energy better expended on the main walk.

View west along the border ridge from below Kasprowy Wierch

After the exciting ride up from Kuźnice, exit from the **cable car station** at **Kasprowy Wierch** and **start the walk**: follow the broad trail straight ahead to an unsignposted junction and turn right to follow the red-waymarked route. The path crosses the steep

Border ridge path past Suche Czuby (left) and on the flanks of Goryczkowa Czuba (below)

southern slope of Kasprowy Wierch, then descends to the first saddle of the day. From here the peak looming above is, mercifully, bypassed on the southern (Slovakian) side, along a narrow path above the steep grassy mountainside. This takes you to a col at 1801m. There follows a short ascent part way up **Goryczkowa Czuba (55min)**. An excellent, if slender path leads on well below the summit, negotiates one rock outcrop and takes you to another, small col. From here you descend to skirt the next outcrop, **Suche Czuby**.

From here there is a rocky descent to a dip (**1h12min**), beyond which you quickly pass a first rock pinnacle, go through a tiny gap, then pass a second pinnacle. Then you rise slightly, for a short stroll along the crest. The path passes below the next peak, **Suchy Wierch Kondracki**, and reaches a path junction high above the refuge shown on page 56, Schronisko na Kondratowej Hali (**1h42min**). (Note: The green-waymarked route leading north at this point could provide an escape route down to the refuge if necessary, but I can't offer a first-hand description, other than to say it looks straightforward and not too steep.)

Climb steadily from here to the summit of **Kondracka Kopa** (**2h2min**). Apart from the marvellous panoramic view, there's a marked change in the character of the mountains as far as you can see southwestwards: pinnacles and crags give way to broader, more evenly contoured ridges and spurs. *(After visiting this summit, the Shorter walk descends the yellow-waymarked route.)*

Drop down to the next gap, from where it's not too steep an ascent to the broad, flat summit of **Małołaczniak** (**2h30min**), and a magnificent view of most of the Tatra Mountains to the east. (A blue-waymarked route descends steeply northwestwards from here.) There follows a short downhill section and a fairly easy ascent to the highest point on the walk, the rock-strewn summit of **Krzesanica** (2122m; **2h52min**), for an even better vista, taking in Zakopane's valley and the Gubałówka ridge. The ensuing steepish descent, still with red waymarks, provides awesome views of the cliff-lined amphitheatre below.

Continue up to the amorphous summit of **Ciemniak** (**3h9min**). There is no signpost here, but the red and green waymarks are clear as you change direction to descend from the ridge via a broad spur. At a path junction (**3h39min**) there's a striking view of a narrow gap between two cliffs forming a V above the valley below to the west. Further on, the first low bushes on the walk make you feel almost claustrophobic after hours on open ground (**4h14min**)!

The path veers left off the crest at **Upłaziańska Kopka**, a small tor (**4h27min**), and descends into woodland. It crosses the edge of a meadow, leads into forest and widens into a rocky stream, easily avoided on one side or the other along narrower paths created by rock-weary walkers. Eventually, you cross a bridge and come to a better trail, where you turn left. Two minutes later you meet the unsurfaced road in **Kościeliska Dolina** (**5h20min**); turn right. This makes the last part of the walk pleasantly easy, down the mostly open valley, past a shepherd's cabin and on to **Kiry** (**5h43min**), where you can catch a service bus or find a minibus waiting.

Walk 7 (Polish High Tatras): THE ASCENT OF ORNAK

See map on pages 64-65; see also photograph on page 1
Distance: 22.2km/13.8mi; 6h55min
Grade: strenuous (1026m/3365ft ascent); on signposted and waymarked paths, trails, tracks, unsurfaced roads and a quiet road
Equipment: see page 31
Refreshments: available at Kiry (the start), at Schronisko na Hali Ornak and at Siwa Polana; fresh water is available en route as indicated. There are toilets at the start and at intervals along the valley road from there.
Transport: see Walk 5, page 54; then bus to Kiry and back from Siwa Polana (see Transport, page 133). Buses leave from opposite Zakopane bus station. There are car parking areas at the start and finish of the walk if you can arrange private transport between them (!): Kiry is on route 958 (the Zakopane/Czarny Dunajec road) approximately 7km southwest of central Zakopane. The turnoff to Siwa Polana is clearly signposted, 2.3km further northwest along route 958 as *Dolina Chochołowska;* the car park is 0.9m along the minor road. Note: cycles can be hired when you reach Chochołowska Dolina, saving 5.5km walking down to Siwa Polana.
Nearest accommodation: Zakopane
Shorter walk: Chochołowska Dolina direct. 15.5km/9.6mi; 4h. Moderate, with 532m/1745ft ascent. Equipment, refreshments and transport as for main walk. Follow the main walk to the 2h11min-point, then continue on the yellow-waymarked route (steeply down in places). On coming to a junction (2h51min), follow the main walk from the 5h40min-point to the end.

This, the longest walk described in the Polish Tatras, rewards your efforts with superb mountain views and fine valley scenery. The highest point reached, Zadni Ornak (1867m, but bypassed on the Shorter walk), affords magnificent vistas of the border ridge in particular. Chochołowska Dolina, the valley to which you descend, draws its fair share of crowds but, as elsewhere in the Tatras, it's easy to feel that the overwhelming majority of people, nearly all Polish, come here because they enjoy being in the mountains and are proud of their heritage.

Set out from **Kiry** along the unsurfaced road (green waymarks) leading directly south into **Kościeliska Dolina**. You pass a shepherd's hut, path junctions, a small **oratory** (**21min**) and more path junctions. Then the road leads through a small gorge where it's freezing cold early in the morning, so the picnic tables at the meadows, **Pisana Polana** (**45min**) are most welcome on a sunny day. The road crosses and recrosses a stream, **Kościeliski Potok**, and passes through another chilly small gorge where sundry paths lead left and right to various caves. Having gained some height, the road reaches the open meadow of **Smytnia Polana** (**1h10min**), with good views of cliffs high above to the northwest. Continue up, past more path junctions on the left, to **Schronisko na Hali Ornak** (**1h15min**).

From this refuge follow the yellow-waymarked path, across a nearby stream and then a small meadow with a picnic table, to the

View west from Pisana Polana to Kominiarski Wierch, with the Kościeliski stream nearby

start of the ascent. Stepping stones then simplify two minor stream crossings (**1h33min** and another a few minutes further on). A steep climb takes you up to open ground at a pass, **Iwaniacka Przełęcz** (**2h11min**), from where there is an impressive view of the cliffs of Kominiarski Wierch above to the north. *(The Shorter walk descends the yellow-waymaked route here.)*

Continue south from the pass along the green-waymarked route, at first through tall conifers. Soon you're among dwarf pines, with a fine view east to Ciemniak on the border ridge (Walk 6). A sharp right bend (**2h38min**) marks the start of the uncompromising ascent towards the crest of the spur, where uninterrupted magnificent views dictate a rest (**3h8min**). Beyond a slight dip, the path rises to cross the craggy summit of **Ornak** (**3h22min**), though you can bypass it on the left (eastern) side. Continue down to a small col then steeply up over the next knoll and up again, scrambling easily to the high point of the walk, the summit of **Zadni Ornak** (**3h47min**). The prospect generally southwards to the border ridge is dominated by the huge bulk of Błyszcz — a pronunciation challenge, if nothing else!

Descend via a minor peak to **Siwa Przełęcz** (**4h8min**). From this pass continue down the path traversing the slope, descending ever more steeply, beside a stream for a while (two fresh water sources, but water purifying tablets may be advisable). The gradient slackens as the path swings away from the stream (**4h40min**). The going becomes easier when you join an old track (**5h12min**) which leads down into **Starorobociańska Dolina**. Pass a junction on the right (**5h40min**; *the Shorter walk joins here*) and continue down the track. With a wide unsurfaced road in sight, bear right at a fork to reach it (**5h48min**).

Press on, now down **Chochołowska Dolina**, soon passing (or being waylaid by) cycles for hire: you could ride down to Siwa Polana and return the cycle there. It's easy walking down the wide road through the forested valley to **Polana Huciska** (**6h10min**; Picnic 7), a hive of activity. Cycles can be hired here too, and this meadow is the terminus of the local 'bus' — a dressed-up tractor pulling two carriages, which could carry you back to the start for a very modest fare (half-hourly service). Horses and carts, their drivers in traditional garb, also operate along the road to Siwa Polana, though for rather larger fees. The road leads on through conifer forest, eventually bursting into the open at the start of **Siwa Polana** (**6h42min**), dotted with chalets old and new and with the **bus stop and car park** at the far end (**6h55min**).

Walk 8 (Polish High Tatras): A RIDGE WALK ABOVE CHOCHOŁOWSKA DOLINA

See also photos on pages 2, 11
Distance: 21.5km/13.3mi; 6h30min
Grade: moderate-strenuous (approximately 880m/2890ft ascent) on a waymarked road, unsurfaced road, tracks, trail and paths; signposted intermittently
Equipment: see page 31
Refreshments: available at Siwa Polana and Schronisko na Chochołowskiej Polanie (where there are also toilets). Water bottles can be replenished in Jarząbcza Dolina.
Transport: see Walk 5, page 54; then 🚘 or 🚌 to Siwa Polana. Buses leave from opposite Zakopane bus station (see Transport, page 133). Travelling by car, from Zakopane follow route 958 (the Zakopane/Czarny Dunajec road) generally south and west for 7km, to the minor road signposted *Dolina Chochołowska;* it's 0.9km to the car park (on the left). From the national park entrance, a 'bus' — a dressed-up tractor pulling two carriages, plies the valley road as far as Polana Huciska (3.5km); costing only pence, it runs half-hourly from 8am. Horses and carts, their drivers in traditional garb, also operate along the road to Polana Huciska, though for rather larger fares.
Nearest accommodation: Zakopane
Shorter walk: Schronisko na Chochołowskiej Polanie. 15.2km/9.4mi; 3h40min. Easy-moderate (approximately 260m/850ft ascent). Equipment, refreshments (except for the water source) and transport as for the main walk. Follow the main walk to the 1h13min-point, then continue along the unsurfaced road to the refuge *(Schronisko)*. It's a 25-minute walk if you go straight there, but you may want to diverge to visit a chapel overlooking Chochołowska Polana, in which case pick up the main walk

at the 4h35min-point. From the refuge retrace steps to Siwa Polana. Shorter versions still could take advantage of the 'bus' to and from Polana Huciska, saving 7km; alternatively, cycles can be hired for the ride down to Siwa Polana, either just north of the path junction (30min down from the refuge) and saving 5.5km, or at Polana Huciska, saving 3.5km.

Optional side trip: Kończysty Wierch. 3km;1.9mi; 1h30min; 264m/870ft ascent. From **Trzydniowianski Wierch** (the 2h52min-point), a clear path with green waymarks leads southeast then south along the spur, skirting the peak Czubik, to a distinct gap; it then climbs steeply to the summit of **Kończysty Wierch**, just on the border (**47min**). Retrace steps to **Trzydniowianski Wierch** (**1h30min**).

Pope John Paul II enjoyed walking in the Tatra Mountains in his younger days; much later he returned to the area featured in this walk, and a path has been named in his honour. The route also includes an ascent to a particularly scenic high point in the western reaches of the national park. An optional side trip to Kończysty Wierch on the border ridge is suggested — well worth the effort.

Starting from **Siwa Polana**, the first part of the walk is simple: follow the road to **Polana Huciska**, where the mountains come enticingly into view (**40min**; Picnic 7). Continue from this meadow along the unsurfaced road through the forested valley, to the third junction beyond Polana Huciska, signposted to *Trzydniowianski Wierch* and waymark in red (**1h13min**). Bear left here. *(But for the Shorter walk, keep straight on.)* At first the route switches between a path and a narrow logging track; at a fork (**1h18min**) bear right to climb very steeply straight up the valley. After a while, follow the waymarks to the left (**1h38min**), across the valley.

Eventually you reach the crest of the spur (**2h18min**), where the path is, in places, partly hidden by intertwined dwarf pine roots. Not a moment too soon, it leads out into open grassland (**2h34min**) which makes for delightfully easy walking up to the knobbly summit of **Trzydniowianski Wierch** (**2h52min**). Among much else, Giewont (Walk 5) can be seen. *(The Optional side-trip diverges here.)*

The red-waymarked path down from here isn't signposted but is clearly defined, descending southwards, then bending sharp

Chochołowska Polana

POLAND
SLOVAKIA
Siwa Polana
Cisowa Turnia
1112
Zadnia Rosocha
1271
Chochołowska Dolina
Polana Huciska
P
1 km
1 mi
0
Bobrowiec
1668
Hrubas
1499
Kominiarski Wierch
1829
Kaplica Święty Jana Chrzciciela
Schronisko na Chochołowskiej Polanie
Chochołowska Polana
Starorobociańska Dolina
Iwaniaka Przełęcz
Szlak Jana Pawła II
Jarząbczy Potok
Jarząbcza Dolina
Trzydniowianski Wierch
1758
Ornak
1854
1867
Zadni Ornak
Czubik
1846
1840
Kotłowa Czubka
1812
Siwa Przełęcz
Kończysty Wierch
1954
2178
Srarorobociański Wierch
SLOVAKIA
Błyszcz 2159

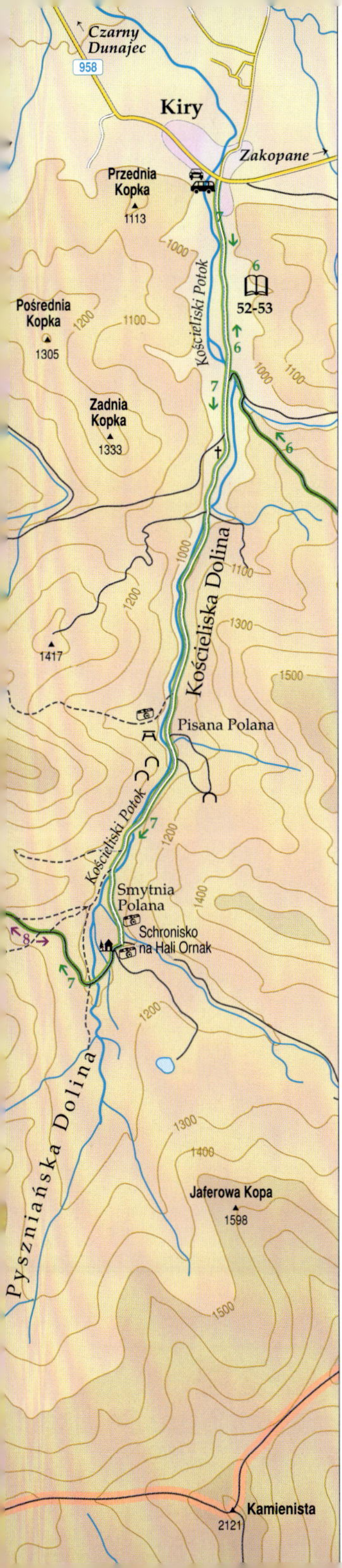

right to drop steeply into the valley, **Jarząbcza Dolina**. The gradient eases once the path starts to zigzag (**3h20min**), crossing two small streams then diving into conifer forest (**3h37min**). Descend steeply to a footbridge across **Jarząbczy Potok** (**3h56min**) and continue down a broad trail to a railed path on the right (**4h2min**). A short distance along the path is a **shrine** visited and blessed by Pope John Paul II; perhaps equally memorable is the view of the spur from which you've recently descended. Continue down the valley on a track, named 'Szlak Jana Pawla II', which soon widens and leads on through a small meadow (picnic table) and on to the much more extensive meadow of **Chochołowska Polana** (**4h35min**). Opposite you is the signposted path up to **Kaplica Święty Jana Chrzciciela**. Beside the tiny wooden chapel (**4h40min**; photograph page 2) is a large cross commemorating John Paul's visit in 1983.

Continue to the left, slightly uphill, then down to the cobbled trail to **Schronisko na Chochołowskiej Polanie** (**4h44min**). On the wall to the left of the steps to the main entrance is a plaque recalling the clandestine meeting here between John Paul II and Lech Wałęsa (leader of the Solidarity Movement and later President of Poland) in 1983. Another plaque beside the door records that John Paul was made an Honorary Tatras Guide at that time. The bar-restaurant (with a Polish-only menu) is to the left.

To return, set off down the cobbled path and across the beautiful meadow; shortly, local goats' cheese may be for sale at a cabin on the left. Continue past the junction with your outgoing path (**5h7min**), through **Polana Huciska** (**5h50min**), and back to **Siwa Polana** (**6h30min**).

Walk 9 (Polish High Tatras): A LAKES TOUR

Distance: 14.3km/8.9mi; 4h50min

Grade: moderate-strenuous (approximately 890m/2920ft ascent); on signposted and waymarked paths and trails

Equipment: see page 31

Refreshments: available at Kuźnice and Schronisko Murowaniec

Transport: (Car tours 1 and 7), or to Zakopane (see page 50), then car or bus to Kuźnice. Those travelling by bus can either use a regular service or private minibus; return by private minibus (see Transport, page 133). Motorists: the car park nearest the walk is very small — it's 1km north of Kuźnice, near the junction of Ulica P Tatrzańskich and Ulica M Karłowicza (see the town plan).

Nearest accommodation: Zakopane

Shorter walks

1 Schronisko Murowaniec. 9.4km/5.8mi; 3h. Easy-moderate, with 474m/1555ft ascent. Equipment, refreshments and transport as for the main walk. Follow the main walk to this refuge (the 1h14min-point); retrace steps to **Wielka Królowa Kopa** and follow the main walk route from the 3h45min-point to **Kuźnice**.

2 Czarny Staw Gąsienicowy. 12.4km/7.7mi; 3h45min. Moderate (594m/1950ft ascent). Equipment, refreshments and transport as for

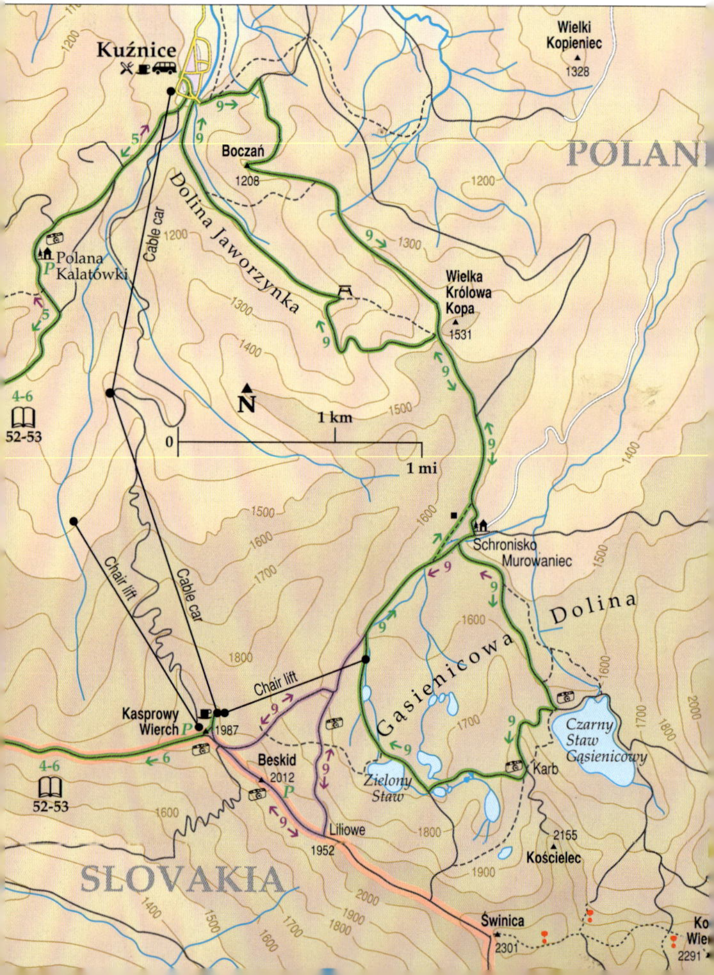

the main walk. Follow the main walk to this lake (the 1h44min-point), then retrace steps past **Schronisko Murowaniec** to **Wielka Królowa Kopa**. Pick up the main walk here and follow the notes from the 3h45min-point to return to **Kuźnice**.

3 Kasprowy Wierch. 6.9km/4.3mi; 2h30min. Easy (minimal ascent; approximately 960m/3150ft descent). Equipment and refreshments as for main walk; refreshments are also available at Kasprowy Wierch. Transport: 🚡 from Kuźnice to Kasprowy Wierch (see Transport, page 133). First, visit the summit: exit from the cable car station and climb steps to the right, past a large building and along to the summit of **Kasprowy Wierch**, for an excellent view of the western Tatras, Giewont (Walk 5) and much else. Return to the station entrance and walk down the steps, then follow a wide trail straight ahead to an unmarked junction. Turn left here; the broad path (yellow waymarks) soon descends steeply, past a junction on the right, to a signposted junction with a black-waymarked route. Join the main walk here, at the 3h2min-point, to return to **Kuźnice**.

Optional side trip: Border ridge and Beskid. 3.5km/2.2mi; 1h50min. Easy-moderate, with 404m/1325ft ascent. From the 3h2min-point in the main walk, turn left up a cobbled path to an unsignposted junction on a bend to the right; bear left here (green waymarks), soon passing a good viewpoint on the left, then another one (**8min**). Climb steadily, then steeply to the border ridge at the saddle of **Liliowe** (**35min**). Turn right, soon ascending sharply to the pinnacle of **Beskid** (2012m) and even more superb views (**49min**). Go on to the major (but unmarked) junction below **Kasprowy Wierch** and the **cable car station** to the right (**1h4min**); turn right and descend to rejoin the main walk at the 3h2min-point.

Alternative walk: Border ridge direct. 15km/9.3mi; 6h. Moderate-strenuous, with 987m/3240ft ascent. Equipment, refreshments and transport as for the main walk. Follow the main walk to the **refuge** at the 1h14min-point, then continue along the yellow-waymarked route towards Kasprowy Wierch. After 35 minutes, join the **optional side trip** described above at an unsignposted junction. Follow the green route south, to the border ridge at the saddle of **Liliowe** and go on to **Beskid**. Descend to rejoin the main walk at the 3h2min-point and return to **Kuźnice**.

There is much more to the Tatra National Park than towering peaks and spiky ridges. Several alpine tarns (mountain lakes), accessible with comparative ease, lie below these rugged features, their serenity contrasting wonderfully with their dramatic surroundings. As well as sampling these lakes, this walk visits one of the very popular remote mountain inns where you can enjoy drinks and traditional local fare. Three shorter walks are outlined above, plus an optional side trip up to the Polish-Slovak border ridge, and an alternative walk to that same high point.

Starting at **Kuźnice**, walk past the shops, cross a bridge, pay the park fee and bear left to follow the blue-waymarked route to *Hala Gąsienicowa*. Cross another bridge and go up a steep cobbled

Gąsienicowa Dolina lakes

trail, then turn right at a junction (**8min**). The grade eases briefly around a hill, **Boczań,** and a sharp left bend. Soon you emerge from the forest (**24min**); the path climbs steadily now, with good views, to a small gap, then traverses a low hill and leads up to a path junction below **Wielka Królowa Kopa** (**46min**).

Continue with the blue route, traversing another spur, then descend to a meadow dotted with small wooden chalets. At its southern end is the large, very popular **Schronisko Murowaniec** (**1h14min**). *(Shorter walk 1 returns from this refuge.)*

To continue, follow blue waymarks towards *Zawrat;* after two minutes bear left at a junction and follow a cobbled path through dwarf pines then up to the shore of **Czarny Staw Gąsienicowy** and a path junction (**1h44min**). Contrasts are the essence of the scene — the tranquil lake and reflections of the surrounding angular peaks. *(Shorter walk 2 returns from here.)*

Follow the black- and green-waymarked route to the right, through dwarf pines and across a boulder field, then rising fairly steeply up to a narrow spur (**2h6min**). From here the path drops slightly to a gap at a junction called **Karb** (**2h16min**). Here you leave the black route to those brave enough to scale the seemingly vertical side of Kościelec soaring above. Descend westwards via the blue route into the valley **Gąsienicowa Dolina**, speckled with tarns large and small. Water bottles can be replenished from a hollowed-out log beside the path (**2h32min**). Soon you cross a stream on stepping stones, then go on to a path junction (**2h44min**). Turn right, now with black waymarks, and soon you pass the largest of the tarns, **Zielony Staw**. Continue to the next junction, about 100m beyond a small **chair lift** (**3h2min**). *(Shorter walk 3 joins here, and the Optional side trip turns left here.)*

Turn right along the yellow-waymarked path; from a minor, unsignposted junction (**3h13min**) you can bypass Schronisko Murowaniec: follow a narrow but clear path past a small **weather station** to another junction, and go on to join the blue-waymarked path (**3h22min**). Otherwise, stay on the yellow path to the refuge, then follow the blue route for Kuźnice from there.

Follow the well-trodden path up to a crest, then down to **Wielka Królowa Kopa** (**3h45min**). Turn left here along another yellow-waymarked path, heading down a steep-sided spur into a valley, **Dolina Jaworzynka**. A good way down, on a sharp left bend, there's a thoughtfully provided **picnic table** (**4h17min**). The gradient is kinder from here, as you walk down through pleasant meadows. Benches outside rustic **log cabins** are temping for a short rest before the last stage, along a trail through conifer forest, back to **Kuźnice** (**4h50min**).

Walk 10 (Polish High Tatras): THE VALLEY OF THE FIVE POLISH LAKES AND MORSKIE OKO

See also photographs on pages 12 (top) and 50
Distance: 19.6km/12.1mi; 6h15min
Grade: moderate-strenuous (approximately 895m/2940ft ascent); on signposted and waymarked roads, trails and paths. There is a short descent with chain on the approach to Morskie Oko, but the passage is *not* exposed or difficult.
Equipment: see page 31
Refreshments: available at Polana Palenica, Schronisko Gorskie, Schronisko przy Morskim Oku and Włosienica
Transport: 🚗 (Car tours 1 and 7), 🚆 or 🚌 to Zakopane (see page 50), then car or bus to Polana Palenica. Buses for Polana Palenica leave from opposite Zakopane bus station; most of the relevant minibuses display the destination sign 'Morskie Oko' (see Transport, page 133). Travelling by car, from Zakopane drive northeast on route 47, the main road to Nowy Targ and Kraków. At a major junction at Poronin (6.5km), turn right along route 961 and continue east through a string of semi-rural villages to a junction at Bukowina Tatrzańska (16.5km). Turn right on route 960 towards Łysa Polana; the road climbs to a junction (26.5km) close to the Polish/Slovak border, where you turn right for 1.5km along a minor road to the large (pay) parking area at Polana Palenica.
Nearest accommodation: Zakopane
Shorter walks
1 Wielki Staw Polski. 15km/9.3mi; 4h30min. Moderate (approximately 700m/2300ft ascent). Equipment and transport as for the main walk; refreshments available at Polana Palenica and Schronisko Gorskie. Follow the main walk to **Wielki Staw Polski**, the 2h23min-point, from where the Gorskie refuge is only 10min away, then retrace steps to Polana Palenica.
2 Morskie Oko. 15.2km/9.4mi; 3h45min. Easy (422m/1385ft ascent). Equipment and transport as for the main walk; refreshments available at Polana Palenica, Schronisko przy Morskim Oku and Włosienica. Follow the main walk to the 35min-point. Continue up the road, taking red-waymarked short cuts (27min, 50min), to the lake, **Morskie Oko** (**2h**). See Optional side trips below.
Optional side trips
1 Circuit of Morskie Oko. 2.3km/1.4mi; 55min. Easy, with minimal ascent; on signposted and waymarked paths. From **Schronisko przy Morskim Oku**

Dolina Roztoki and the Wołoszyn ridge, from the 3h19min-point

descend steps to the lake shore and bear left along a red-waymarked path. It wanders up and down, rarely without a lake view, past an unsignposted but prominent junction on the left (**28min**; see Side trip 2 below), through pines and mountain ash, back to the refuge.

2 Czarny Staw pod Rysami. 1.2km/0.7mi; 45min. Easy, with 188m/617ft ascent on a steep, well-made path. From the 28min-point on the Morskie Oko circuit path (Side trip 1 above), follow the red-waymarked path. It climbs, steeply in places, to the shore of another lake, **Czarny Staw pod Rysami** (**23min**), overlooked by the soaring mass of rock that is Rysy (2499m) — Poland's highest peak, tapering to a pinnacle and flanked by a crinkly ridge to the east and a bulkier massif to the west.

Retrace steps to Morskie Oko and turn left.

The Valley of the Five Polish Lakes (Dolina Pieciu Stawow Polskich) and Morskie Oko, another beautiful lake, in the eastern reaches of the national park, are two of the best known and most visited places in the Polish Tatras, and for good reason. You can expect to share the latter part of the walk with many others, but I hope this experience doesn't diminish your enjoyment. Two optional side trips are described: a circuit of the famous Morskie Oko, and to Czarny Staw pod Rysami above it.

Start the walk from **Polana Palenica**: set out along the road (closed to public traffic) leading southwest; it gains some height and provides occasional fine views eastwards to some craggy peaks. On the far side of the bridge over the **river Roztoka**, you come to a junction (**35min**; *Shorter walk 2 continues along the road from here*). Take a few steps to the right, up the green-waymarked, cobbled trail, then bear left up wide stone steps. Now an undulating path through the forest takes you across a wide **bridge** (**47min**) and on to a **picnic shelter** (**1h17min**) where the grandeur of **Dolina Roztoki** unfolds, enclosed by rugged, steep-sided ridges.

A short distance past the second of two **footbridges** close together (**1h21min**), bear right uphill. The path climbs steadily and passes under an aerial cableway. Walk past a turn-off left to Schronisko Gorskie (**1h45min**) and continue steeply up, past **Siklawa** — the long waterfall spilling over the rim. With the top of the ascent in sight, negotiate an easily-angled rock slab with the help of plentiful small niches, and soon you reach the edge of **Wielki Staw Polski** (**2h23min**), the largest of the five lakes. *(Shorter Walk 1 returns from here.)*

Bear left along the blue-waymarked path; there's a fine vantage point a few minutes further on, between Wielki Staw and the pond-sized **Mały Staw** (**2h27min**). Continue to the superbly sited **Schronisko Gorskie**, overlooking **Przedni Staw Polski** (**2h33min**).

From this refuge, stay with the blue waymarks, as you continue along the lake shore, cross boulder fields, then rise directly above **Dolina Roztoki** to the crest of the spur enclosing the eastern side of the valley (**3h19min**). From here four of the lakes are clearly in view, and the basin of the fifth easily discernible. The route descends, crosses a boulder field, then rises to the crest of the spur ahead; there's a wonderful vantage point below **Kepa** a short distance further on (**3h43min**).

From here descend steadily into the valley, **Dolina Rybiego Potoku**, generally on a good path, apart from a short crumbly stretch easily passable with the help of a chain handrail (**4h10min**). When you come to a road (**4h30min**) turn right to reach **Morskie Oko** and **Schronisko przy Morskim Oku** (**4h38min**). It's most likely that you'll have to join a queue for refreshments. See optional side trips above.

The return is straightforward: back down the road, past **Włosienica** (**4h58min**; toilets, picnic tables) to the first of the succession of short cut paths across wide bends in the road (**5h12min**). You pass the junction of your outward route (**5h42min**) and are soon back in **Polana Palenica** (**6h15min**).

SLOVAKIA'S TATRA NATIONAL PARK

Slovakia's Tatra National Park (Tatranský Národný Park; Walks 11-19) was set aside in 1949 and protects 79,513ha/196,475 acres of the High Tatras range, Slovakia's only truly alpine mountains. Glaciation was the major force in shaping the High Tatras, which comprise three distinct regions: the central High Tatras (predominantly granite), the western High Tatras (west of Liliowe Sedlo, see Walk 9), and the Belianske Tatras (east of Kopské Sedlo; see Walk 19), both of which are mostly limestone. Forests of spruce and various pine species, and beech and maple (mainly on limestone) extend from approximately 800m up to the main tree line at 1550m. Above that height, meadows and extensive tracts of dwarf pine reach up beyond 2000m. Of five major peaks, Gerlachovský Štít (2655m) is supreme; two others, Kriváň and Slavkovský Štít, are featured in this guide (Walks 14 and 16).

Visitors have been coming to Slovakia's High Tatras since the late 19th century, when spa or health resorts were founded, first at Štrbské Pleso, then Starý Smokovec and Tatranská Lomnica. Some 600km/370miles of signposted and waymarked paths and trails bring the valleys, with their beautiful lakes, and some of the peaks within reach of reasonably fit walkers. The several mountain inns or chalets *(chaty)*, where food and drink are provided, are another enticement. The national park's museum in Tatranská Lomnica (see plan on the reverse of the touring map) is open Mon-Fri and weekend mornings; although the display captions are in Slovak only, it is well worth a visit. The park's website, www.tanap.org, has an informative English-language section, including details of the paths which are closed between 1 November and 15 June. For accommodation and transport information, log on to www.tatry.sk.

The large town of Poprad is the main transport centre for the park. It lies on the railway line between Košice (Slovakia's second city) in the east, Spišská Nová Ves (Slovenský Raj), Liptovský Mikuláš (Low Tatras), Žilina (Malá Fatra) and Bratislava; some services continue to Prague. Trains depart daily at least hourly, more frequently between 10am and early evening. Daily long-distance SAD buses serve the same towns with comparable frequency; there is also a daily service Poprad/Zakopane (for Poland's Tatra National Park), usually departing at 10.05 and 16.50 from June to September. Alternatively, SAD operates a daily service to Łysa Polana on the Polish border (via Starý Smokovec and Tatranská Lomnica) which generally connects with PKS buses to Zakopane; from Poprad there are four departures daily, another four from 1/7-31/8. See transport details for Walks 11-19 on pages 133-134.

Walk 11 (Slovakian High Tatras): POPRADSKÉ PLESO AND VEL'KÉ HINCOVO PLESO

Distance: 14.6km/9.1mi; 5h
Grade: moderate (700m/2300ft ascent); on signposted and waymarked roads, trails and paths
Equipment: see page 31
Refreshments: available at Chata Popradské Pleso and Štrbské Pleso
Transport: 🚗 (Car tours 3 and 5; park in one of the designated car parks), 🚂 or 🚌 to Štrbské Pleso (see page 72 and Transport, page 133). See **plan** of Štrbské Pleso on the reverse of the touring map.
Nearest accommodation: Štrbské Pleso

Shorter walk: Popradské Pleso. 8km/4.8mi; 2h15min. Easy-moderate (250m/820ft ascent). Equipment, refreshments and transport as for the main walk. Follow the main walk to a junction (**Rázcestie nad Popradskýn Plesom**; **1h9min**), then cross the road and walk down the path to the lake. Do at least one of the optional **side-trips** (below), then retrace steps to **Štrbské Pleso**.

Optional side-trips

1 Circuit of Popradské Pleso. 1.3km/0.8mi; 25min. Easy; negligible ascent. From the junction (**Rázcestie nad Popradskýn Plesom**; 1h9min or 3h50min), cross the road and walk down the path to the lake shore. Turn left to pass (and/or patronise) **Chata Popradské Pleso**, and continue along a clear path close to the shore, across two footbridges and past a signposted turnoff to distant destinations. Soon you're treated to marvellous views all the way up Dolina to the border ridge. Just past the signposted turnoff for the cemetery (**15min**; Symbolický Cintorín; see below) cross a **footbridge** over the lake's outlet stream. Within a minute you come to well-placed picnic benches. Continue on the path, through forest, past an unsigned junction, and back to the road just below the junction, **Rázcestie nad Popradskýn Plesom**, then return to **Štrbské Pleso**.

2 Symbolický Cintorín. 1km/0.6mi; 15min. Easy (approximately 25m/80ft ascent). From the **junction at the 15min-point in side-trip 1** above, follow the yellow-waymarked path. It dips, then rises quite steeply through forest. A **sign** by the path (**6min**) shows the layout of the area. Continue up to a small wooden-roofed **chapel** (**8min**), pay the modest fee and obtain an informative leaflet about the **cemetery** (English translation available). Retrace steps to the lakeside path (**15min**).

Vel'ké Hincovo Pleso, the largest and deepest of the many glacial tarns in the High Tatras valleys, makes a very worthwhile objective for a day's outing from Štrbské Pleso. It lies at the head of the beautiful Mengusovská Dolina, almost surrounded by a magnificent array of cliff-lined spurs and spiky peaks, some on the Slovakia-Poland border ridge. Two routes lead to Popradské Pleso from a junction at the 24min-point: the red-waymarked one is vastly superior for scenery and underfoot conditions and is the only one described here. Both optional side trips are highly recommended, for the views across Popradské Pleso, and for the serenity and moving atmosphere of the colourful crosses and the many and varied plaques — memorials to mountaineers — in Symbolický Cintorín in the forest near Popradské Pleso.

Štrbské Pleso (see also photograph on page 10)

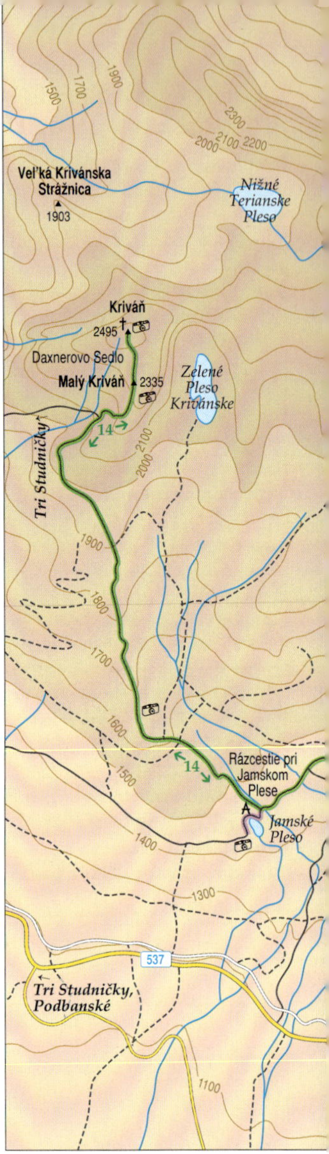

Starting in **Štrbské Pleso** from the **upper car park**, walk up the road towards the mountains, going under a **footbridge**. Almost immediately, turn right (where a clutch of national **park signs** indicates various waymarked routes). Follow the red route and within 200m continue straight ahead at a junction, into the forest. Here an illustrated **information board** introduces a nature trail (in Slovak only). The clearly defined trail climbs steadily through conifer forest to a junction (**24min**); continue straight ahead with red waymarks. The character of the forest begins to change as mountain ash and birch appear and views soon start to open up (**30min**). The superbly designed path follows a more or less level route into **Mengusovská Dolina**, affording ever finer views up the valley and eastwards. It descends (**58min**) to a footbridge then rises to a junction, **Rázcestie nad Popradskýn Plesom** (**1h9min**). *(The Short walk continues to the right here; see also optional side-trips above.)*

Continue up the valley from the junction on a blue-waymarked path, which soon starts to rise as the tall conifers retreat and dwarf pines take over (**1h23min**). Cross a footbridge over a small stream and you soon come to another junction, **Rázcestie nad Zabím Potokom** (**1h31min**). Press on along the blue path, soon descending slightly to cross two streams on broad flattish boulders (**1h39min**). The steady ascent continues, steepening beyond a sharp bend to the right, as you rise up the side of a broad spur and then continue along the crest.

You come onto a plateau strewn with rocks encrusted with lime-green lichen and a few flattened dwarf pines. It's easy going now, to the shore of **Vel'ké Hincovo Pleso (2h36min)**. The best vantage points are on slightly higher ground to the east, across the outlet stream, or from higher ground nearby to the west.

Start to retrace your steps down **Mengusovská Dolina** but, after about three minutes, head off to the right across grassland for a view of the small secluded lake, Malé Hincovo Pleso.

Back at **Rázcestie nad Popradskýn Plesom (3h50min)**, bear right to retrace your outgoing route all the way back to **Štrbské Pleso (5h)**. However, if you didn't take the side-trips on the way out, it would be a great shame not to do them now!

Walk 12 (Slovakian High Tatras): PREDNÉ SOLISKO AND FURKOTSKÁ DOLINA

See map on pages 74-75; see also photos on pages 10, 74
Distance: 7.6km/4.7mi; 3h10min
Grade: easy-moderate (approximately 275m/900ft ascent and 740m/2425ft descent); on waymarked paths, trails and tracks
Equipment: see page 31
Refreshments: available at Chata pod Soliskom (English language menu) and Štrbské Pleso
Transport: , or to Štrbské Pleso, as Walk 11, page 73. Then Solisko chair lift from Štrbské Pleso: to reach the bottom station, walk straight up the road through the village from the upper car park. See **plan** of Štrbské Pleso on the reverse of the touring map.
Nearest accommodation: Štrbské Pleso
Shorter walks
1 Predné Solisko. 1.6km/1mi; 1h10min. Easy (253m/830ft ascent). Equipment, refreshments and transport as for the main walk. Follow the main walk to **Predné Solisko (35min)**, then retrace your steps and return to Štrbské Pleso by chair lift.
2 Furkotská Dolina. 6km/3.7mi; 2h. Easy (minimal ascent and approximately 740m/2425ft descent). Equipment, refreshments and transport as for the main walk. From the chair lift, pick up the main walk at the 1h10min-point and walk down **Furkotská Dolina** to Štrbské Pleso, omitting the ascent of Predné Solisko.
3 Blue route to Štrbské Pleso. 4.1km/2.5mi; 1h50min. Easy (253m/830ft ascent and 740m/2427ft descent). Equipment, refreshments and transport as for the main walk. Follow the **main walk to the 1h10min-point**, then walk down to Štrbské Pleso by using the notes for **Walk 13** from the 5h2min-point (page 80).

This outstandingly scenic walk starts with a spectacular chair lift ride from Štrbské Pleso to a superbly sited *chata* (mountain inn) with sweeping valley views across Štrbské Pleso. There follows a climb to a modest summit (by Tatra standards), which affords marvellous views of rugged peaks, ridges and deep valleys. Then you descend through an attractive, lightly wooded valley. The last part of the return to Štrbské Pleso passes through some areas affected by the storm in November 2004 (see page 91).

Shorter walks 1 and 2 offer the opportunity to split the walk between two days; Short walk 3 describes the path down to Štrbské Pleso as an alternative to the chair lift.

You start from the **top station of the Solisko chair lift**: a few steps from the exit, signs on the railing enclosing **Chata pod Soliskom** indicate the directions for the ascent of Predné Solisko (red waymarks, straight ahead) and for Furkotská Dolina (blue waymarks, to the left; Shorter walk 2). The well-waymarked red route leads up past the *chata*, through dwarf pines, and climbs steeply up the mountainside via stone steps. Views to the east extend to the towering Gerlachovský massif, the highest peak in Slovakia (2654m); then Kriváň (Walk 14) appears, its soaring wedge-shaped peak on the western skyline (**20min**). The gradient eases for the last few minutes up the bare, broad slope, to the small cluster of crags marking the summit of **Predné Solisko** (**35min**; Picnic 9).

In Furkotská Dolina, with Kriváň on the skyline; below: Chata pod Soliskom

Return to the *chata* by the same route (**1h10min**). *(Shorter walks 1 and 3 return to Štrbské Pleso from here — 1 by chair lift, 3 on foot. Shorter walk 2 joins here.)* To continue the main walk, follow the blue-waymarked route immediately below the *chata* westwards. You descend stone steps, then cross the steep slopes of Predné Solisko, strewn with boulder fields and clusters of dwarf pines. The well-made path leads into the valley, **Furkotská Dolina**, and down to a junction, **Rázcestie pod Soliskom** (**1h35min**). There is a pleasant grassy area here, ideal for a break. Continue on the yellow path to the left, down the valley. At first it closely follows the nearby stream, **Furkotský Potok**, then descends fairly steeply through dwarf pines, with some good valley views (including the small town of Važek) and leads into varied conifer forest (**1h59min**). The gradient slackens from a grassy clearing, from where Chata pod Soliskom is visible (2h8min). The path passes through a pocket of storm-damaged trees and soon you reach a trail at a junction, **Rázcestie pod Furkotskou Dolinou** (**2h23min**).

Continue along the trail which, at time of writing, soon became a track (**2h28min**), widened by lorries removing the countless thousands of fallen trees from the surrounding area, devastated by the November 2004 storm. Fortunately it's a comparatively small area, and within about 12 minutes it's behind you.

Further on (**2h58min**), there's a short informal path down to the shore of Štrbské Pleso should you prefer to return to your hotel from here (see Picnic 8 on page 27). Otherwise, continue to a signposted junction at the far corner of the impressive hotel, **Liečebný Dom Solisko** (**3h2min**). A short distance to the right is a **lookout** with fine views over the valley below and extending to the Low Tatras on the horizon. From the signposted junction, bear left to reach the lake shore. For the stations and parking area, continue straight on along the road past the former **Hotel Hviezdoslav** (partly demolished at time of writing). About 50m beyond it, follow a path down to the right for the **bus and train stations** and the **car park** in **Štrbské Pleso** (**3h10min**).

Walk 13 (Slovakian High Tatras): FROM MLYNICKÁ DOLINA TO FURKOTSKÁ DOLINA VIA BYSTRÉ SEDLO

See map on pages 74-75
Distance: 12km/8mi; 5h54min
Grade: strenuous (approximately 1100m/3600ft ascent); on signposted and waymarked roads, unsurfaced roads, tracks, trails and paths. Just above Vodopád Skok, a short traverse of a granite boulder is equipped with a chain handrail and the following ascent of a rocky gully also has a chain. Neither section is at all exposed. The final 20-25m of the ascent to Bystré Sedlo (up a steep, but not exposed rocky gully) also has chains — useful aids for climbing the conveniently placed boulders. The first 5m or so down from this gap is also chained and best tackled facing inwards, but it is *not* exposed. Bystré Sedlo is at 2314m, so please read the panel 'Effects of altitude' on page 32.
Equipment: see page 31
Refreshments: available at Štrbské Pleso, Chata pod Soliskom
Transport: as Walk 11, page 73
Nearest accommodation: Štrbské Pleso
Shorter walks
1 Vodopád Skok. 6.4km/4mi; 2h15min. Moderate (approximately 375m/1230ft ascent). Equipment and transport as for the main walk; refreshments only available in Štrbské Pleso. Follow the main walk up **Mlynická Dolina** to the base of the waterfall, **Vodopád Skok** (1h17min); retrace steps from there.
2 Capie Pleso. 10.4km/6.5mi; 4h30min. Moderate (approximately 720m/2360ft ascent), *but see also 'Grade' for main walk.* Equipment, refreshments and transport as for Shorter walk 1. Follow the main walk up Mlynická Dolina to **Capie Pleso** (2h20min); retrace steps from this lake to Štrbské Pleso.
3 Chata pod Soliskom. 9.5km/5.9mi; 5h2min. Strenuous (approximately 1100m/3600ft ascent); *see also 'Grade' for main walk.* Equipment, refreshments and transport as for the main walk (but return on chair lift from Chata pod Soliskom to Štrbské Pleso: the terminus is at the end of the road, just up from the Hotel FIS). Follow the main walk to **Chata pod Soliskom** (the 5h2min-point) and return by chair lift from there. *Before setting out, check the latest departure time, probably about 4pm.*

The spectacularly rugged ridges and spurs between the deep valleys in the High Tatras look completely impassable, except perhaps by rock climbers. However, routes have been devised to take advantage of steep but safely negotiable slopes from which the smallest of gaps in the otherwise unyielding crests can be crossed. Bystré Sedlo, between Mlynická Dolina and Furkotská Dolina, is one such, just wide enough for one person to stand or sit in — although, surprisingly, without any feeling of exposure. Because the pass is so narrow, the crossing is marked on relevant topographical maps as one-way — to avoid sudden, awkward face-to-face encounters in the pass. Unfortunately this protocol is not advertised on the path signs, so is not universally observed, a fact worth keeping in mind. If all this sounds too daunting, just do Shorter walk 2 up to the head of superb Mlynická Dolina, without any one-way traffic worries!

Starting from the **upper car park** in **Štrbské Pleso**, walk up the road towards the mountains, going under a **footbridge** to a junction with a clutch of **national park signs**. Continue straight up the road ahead (the direction for yellow-waymarked routes). Just past the large **Hotel FIS** on the right (**10min**), opposite the **Solisko chair lift station**, the road becomes unsurfaced, then you're on a track and shortly a trail up through conifer forest. Around a bend, what is now a path crosses the distinct transition from tall conifers to dwarf pines (**42min**). Within three minutes vistas of the valley open up and, soon after, the lowlands come into view. Beyond a short **footbridge** (**57min**), from where the waterfall, Vodopád

Okruhle Pleso in Mlynická Dolina

Skok, can be seen ahead sliding down a broad cliff, the path climbs steadily past a **pool (1h12min)**, to the foot of **Vodopád Skok (1h17min)** and a sign about winter closure of mountain paths. *(Shorter walk 1 returns from here.)*

Continue up beside the fall; traverse a broad granite boulder along a natural line of weakness, perhaps using the chain handrail, then climb a rocky gully where the chain may be helpful. It's easy going then, past the lake, **Pleso nad Skokom (1h31min)** and across two streams via large flat boulders. The well-built path then bends left and leads straight up the valley. You climb through conveniently dissected crags, to reach a small valley where there's a **pond** on the left (**1h55min**), then cross boulder fields and ascend steeply beside a stream to the shore of a lake, **Capie Pleso (2h20min)**. *(Shorter walk 2 returns from here.)*

The onward route threads through the boulder field above the lake, dips, then begins the climb. When you reach a large sprawling **cairn**, keep it on your right, to follow an easy route up, bypassing a **large boulder (2h30min)**. Continue traversing up towards the head of the valley; the direction changes from a broad platform littered with small cairns (**2h47min**): bear left and follow a clear line of man-made steps directly uphill. Almost at the base of the cliffs, bear left across boulders to the final ascent in a sheltered rocky gully; chains are helpful in hauling yourself up the slot that is **Bystré Sedlo (3h9min)**.

Once you've taken in the new vista, dominated by the awesome peak Kriváň, use the chain to manoeuvre down the low crags, then set out on the steep descent. A series of tight bends leads you to a traverse above another lake, **Vyšné Wahlenbergovo Pleso** (named after Goran Wahlenberg, a Swedish botanist who visited the High Tatras in the early 19th century). Continue down via steps and a path into the wide shallow valley, **Furkotská Dolina**. A broad undulating path takes you across grassland to a signposted junction, **Rázcestie pod Soliskom (4h39min)**. Turn left with blue waymarks, to follow a solidly build stone path across boulder fields and up to **Chata pod Soliskom (5h2min)**, with an English menu. *(Shorter walk 3 returns to Štrbské Pleso by chair lift from here.)*

To descend on foot, from the right of the **chair lift station** walk down a clear path paralleling a small **ski tow**. At the end of the tow (**5h24min**) there's a most satisfying view of Mlynická Dolina. On the edge of the conifer forest the waymarked path drops steeply to the right, but a track to the left affords easier walking; the two almost merge further on, beside a small **wooden building (5h31min)**. Here you have a choice, depending on where you want to finish up.

For the more direct route, bear left down an unmarked path through a broad clearing and go around a right-hand bend to the **lower chair lift station (5h44min)** and the road straight down to **Štrbské Pleso** village centre (**5h54min**).

Alternatively, follow the track parallel to the waymarked path and another **ski tow**, down through conifers. Where the track swings left (**5h35min**), continue on the waymarked path a few steps to the right. Steep in places and often stony, it descends through the forest to the shore of **Štrbské Pleso (5h51min)**. See Picnic 8 (page 27) for notes about the lake circuit.

Walk 14 (Slovakian High Tatras): THE ASCENT OF KRIVÁŇ

See map on pages 74-75; see also photos on pages 10, 74
Distance: 19.4km;12mi; 7h15min
Grade: strenuous (approximately 1160m/3800ft ascent); on signposted and waymarked roads, tracks, trails and paths. The uppermost reaches of the ascent involve climbing over boulders, although without any chain handrails; while you do need to use your hands, and the ground is steep, the route is *not* exposed. Please read the advice in 'Effects of altitude' on page 32.
Equipment: see page 31
Refreshments: available in Štrbské Pleso; there are opportunities for refilling water bottles before and after (but not during) the main ascent.
Transport: as Walk 11, page 73; then on foot from Štrbské Pleso
Nearest accommodation: Štrbské Pleso
Shorter walk: Jamské Pleso. 10km/6.2mi; 2h10min. Easy (approximately 100m/330ft ascent). Equipment, refreshments and transport as for the main walk. Follow the main walk to the 1h-point, then continue along the trail for barely two minutes, to the secluded lake, **Jamské Pleso**. From the **picnic shelter** on the western side of the lake, continue up a slight rise for about 25m, for a superb view of Kriváň and its neighbours. Retrace steps to **Štrbské Pleso**.

Kriváň (2495m) is the highest peak in Slovakia's High Tatras that is accessible to walkers without the use of any artificial aids — chains, rungs or pitons. It's a fairly long ascent, steep in many places, but immensely worthwhile. The summit, from which the peak's northern and eastern faces drop sheer into the depths, affords extraordinarily wide views, extending from the Gubałówka ridge above Zakopane (setting for Picnic 3) to the Low Tatra Mountains (Walks 23-25). A through walk would be ideal — ascending via the route from Tri Studničky (10.4km west of Štrbské Pleso) and returning via the route described here. But the link — the western continuation of the trail followed from Štrbské Pleso — was closed at time of writing, and will remain closed until all fallen trees from the November 2004 storm (see page 91)

View towards Kriváň from just below Malý Kriváň

have been removed. Moreover, the current Štrbské Pleso/ Liptovský Mikuláš bus timetable dictates a later start from Tri Studničky than common sense would permit. However, the out-and-back walk described below is by no means tedious or repetitive — the outlook is quite different during the descent.

Start in **Štrbské Pleso** by the southern shore of the eponymous lake. Find the signposted junction on the southern side of the older-style **Solisko Hotel**. Red is the waymark colour for your route: follow the unsurfaced road generally northwestwards. The road, then track, passes through some tracts of forest devastated by the November 2004 storm. You pass a junction on the right, where a path comes in from Furkotská Dolina (**32min**; Walk 12). The track becomes a trail through the forest; it's worth taking advantage of the opportunity to top up your water supply where a small stream beside the track has been partly diverted through a short pipe housed in a wooden structure resembling a dog kennel (**50min**).

Continue to a signposted junction, **Rázcestie pri Jamskom Plese**, with a **picnic shelter** (**1h**). Leave the red route here, to head for Kriváň. *(But for the Shorter walk, continue straight ahead.)*

The path soon crosses a stream via a **footbridge** then climbs steeply through conifer forest which, at length, gives way to dwarf pines (**1h19min**). Another burst of climbing brings you out into the open (**1h29min**), where the magnificent **view** which has suddenly appeared — of towering peaks and deep valleys to the east and west, surely warrants a pause. The path leads on up the spur, then swings right (**1h58min**) across a boulder field and a saddle, to rise steeply across the east-facing slope and back up to

the crest of the spur. It continues by traversing (uphill of course!) all the way across to the western flank, then climbs above a deep, steep-sided valley (where you can see the Tri Studničky path mentioned in the introduction). In places the path is covered by small rockfalls, but it's still easy to follow — up to a signposted junction (**2h40min**).

From here the **ascent consists of three sections**: the **first** (and probably the most difficult, where care in following the waymarks is crucial), is virtually straight up the mountainside, through the boulders and up small clefts. The **second** section (**2h52min**) runs along the crest of the spur, with Štrbské Pleso in view. The route crosses the minor bump of **Malý Kriváň** (**3h7min**), but this can easily be bypassed to the left.

From a minor gap, **Daxnerovo Sedlo**, the remarkably good path continues up on the western flank, across boulder fields, to the start of the final ascent. This **third** section is steep but not exposed, and the route, between boulders and across dissected crags, does call for the use of your hands, but there are no awkward moves. Eventually you are up on the flattish summit of **Kriváň** (**3h37min**), topped with a simple wooden cross.

It may take a while for the scope of the panoramic view to sink in; it includes parts of some of the walks described in the Polish High Tatras, the Low Tatra Mountains to the southwest, and the vast expanse of the plains below —from near Liptovský Mikuláš in the west to Poprad and beyond in the east.

The view also provides a classic geology lesson in the features of a glaciated landscape: hanging valleys, deeply scoured rock faces, and long narrow ridges. You can also see that Kriváň stands on the border between the rugged High Tatras to the east and the more benign, rounded western High Tatras.

The descent is more straight-forward than the ascent, as the waymarks are generally easier to follow down to the first path junction (**4h37min**). The return along the outward route is quite different — almost another walk, with fresh perspectives on the views, and many backward glances to the awesome summit — all the way down to the junction, **Rázcestie pri Jamskom Plese** (**6h**) and back to **Štrbské Pleso** (**7h15min**).

Breathtaking view northeast from the summit of Kriváň, with Nižné Terianske Pleso below

Walk 15 (Slovakian High Tatras): TÉRYHO CHATA

See also photos on pages 14, 88
Distance: 12.7km/7.9mi; 4h32min
Grade: moderate (approximately 800m/2625ft ascent); on signposted and waymarked minor road, tracks, trails and paths
Equipment: see page 31
Refreshments: available at Hrebienok, Zamkovského Chata, Téryho Chata, Rainerova Chata and Bilíkova Chata
Transport: (Car tours 2 and 3), or to Starý Smokovec (see page 72), then funicular railway to Hrebienok (see Transport, page 133). Motorists: there is a car park (fee) about 150m south of the funicular station, adjacent to the prominent copper-roofed Grand Hotel and signposted on the main road no more than 120m west of the junction of the 537 and 534 (the Poprad/Starý Smokovec road). See **plan** of Starý Smokovec on reverse of the touring map.

Nearest accommodation: Hrebienok, Starý Smokovec
Shorter walks
1 Rainerova Chata and Bilíkova Chata. 3.8km/2.3mi; 45min. Easy (approximately 80m/262ft ascent). Equipment, transport and refreshments as main walk (except for the Zamkovského and Téryho *chaty*). Follow the main walk to the 18min-point and turn right towards *Rainerova Chata* (green waymarks), then follow the main walk from the 4h5min-point, back to **Hrebienok**.
2 Zamkovského Chata. 6.1km/3.8mi; 2h. Easy (approximately 260m/850ft ascent). Equipment, transport and refreshments as for the main walk (except for Téryho Chata). Follow the main walk to **Zamkovského Chata** (the 49min-point); then follow the main walk from the 3h35min-point back to **Hrebienok**.

For Slovakian walkers, the several mountain inns or refuges *(chaty)* in the Tatras are magnetic attractions for a day's walk. Téryho Chata, perched at 2015m near the edge of a cliff, is small — and unlikely to be overcrowded (as is the case with some of the lower level inns). It stands in an extremely scenic valley beside a path free of chains and rock scrambling (as far as that point, at least). All these factors make Malá Studená Dolina the most attractive of the valleys within reasonable reach of Starý Smokovec. Should you be tempted, it's worth noting that the yellow-waymarked route onwards from Téryho Chata to Vel'ká Studená Dolina via Priečene Sedlo involves not only chains, but also pitons and rungs!

Start the walk to the right of the hotel opposite the **Hrebienok funicular station** beside a 'tree' of signposts. Follow the red route, a broad trail, into the forest. Pass a signposted junction where 'Rainerova Chata' is to the right (**14min**) and descend through an intersection called **Rázcestie nad Rainerovou Chatou**. Walk down to another junction, where *Rainerova Chata* is signposted to the right along a green-waymarked path (**18min**). *(Shorter walk 1 turns right here.)*

Continue on the red route. Beyond a wide bridge, the trail climbs steadily past an impressive waterfall, **Obrovský Vodopád** (**24min**), and emerges into more open dwarf pine woodland with superb views from a sharp left bend (**33min**). Back in tall forest, it's only a few minutes to a path junction (**48min**); continue more or less straight on towards *Téryho Chata* (green waymarks), and within a minute you reach **Zamkovského Chata** (**49min**), an attractive wooden building. The varied menu is available in English. *(For Shorter walk 2, pick up the notes from the 3h35min-point to continue.)*

To the left of the *chata,* a broad trail, soon a path, leads onwards into **Malá Studená Dolina**. It's not long until the tall conifers start to recede and you're in the open, with a fine view all the way up the valley (**1h5min**). Soon Téryho Chata can be seen, high up at the top of the cliff forming a wall across the valley. The path leads up to the base of the cliff (**1h30min**) and swings left to cross boulder fields and a stream, then climbs beside it. Then you go

En route to Téryho Chata, below Žltá Stena

Zamkovského Chata

up a wide boulder-filled gully below the almost sheer face of a vast blade of rock, **Žltá Stena**. The final stretch is up the steep slope on the right, from the top of which it's only a short distance to **Téryho Chata (2h15min)**. Lomnický Štít soars skywards to the northeast, with Lomnické Sedlo, the distinct low point on the

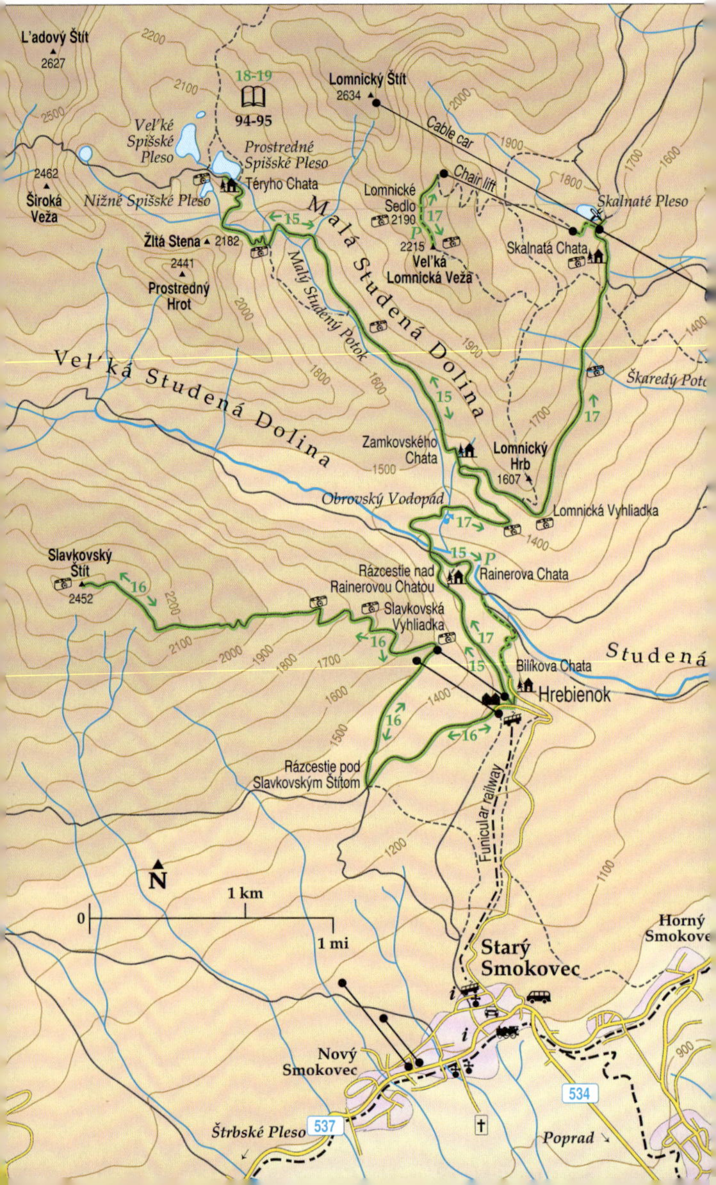

spiky ridge, extending south from the peak. An exploration of the nearby lakes, **Veľké Spišské Pleso** and **Prostredné Spišské Pleso**, as well as **Nižné Spišské Pleso** (hidden below the onward path not far west of the *chata*), is highly recommended. You're spoilt for choice of quiet picnic spots on the grass between the boulders.

Retrace steps, perhaps pausing at a small grassy clearing beside the stream **Malý Studený Potok** (**3h20min**), to **Zamkovského Chata** (**3h35min**). Continue to the nearby path junction and turn right. Descend around a U-bend, past the big waterfall, and across a bridge. At a junction, take the green-waymarked path straight ahead (**4h5min**) to **Rainerova Chata** (**4h8min**; Picnic 10), a small wooden building on the far side of a meadow. Dating from the 1860s, this *chata* was the first to be built. Rather dimly lit, the single room's walls are crowded with photos and assorted climbing equipment. Hot and cold drinks and sweets are available. Continue along the blue- and green-waymarked trail (the trail leading left as you approach the *chata*). It descends, mostly close to the cascading stream, past a junction and on to another, unsignposted junction, where you bear right with green waymarks (**4h18min**). The trail gains height to the hotel-like **Bilíkova Chata** (**4h28min**). Continue up the road ahead briefly, then follow a path on the right up to **Hrebienok** and the **funicular railway station** (**4h32min**).

Walk 16 (Slovakian High Tatras): THE ASCENT OF SLAVKOVSKÝ ŠTÍT

See map on pages 86-87; see also photograph on page 14
Distance: 11.4km/7.1mi; 5h45min
Grade: strenuous (approximately 1180m/3870ft ascent); on signposted and waymarked trails and paths. Slavkovský Štít is at 2452m — please read the advice in the panel 'Effects of altitude' on page 32.
Equipment: see page 31
Refreshments: only available at Hrebienok. *There are no reliable sources of fresh water during the walk,* so carry all you'll need.
Transport: as Walk 15, page 84
Nearest accommodation: Hrebienok, Starý Smokovec
Shorter walk: Slavkovská Vyhliadka. 4.8km/3mi; 1h32min. Easy-moderate (approximately 260m/850ft ascent). Equipment, refreshments and transport as for the main walk. Follow the main walk to the 47min-point — **Slavkovská Vyhliadka**, an exceptionally scenic lookout; retrace steps from there to **Hrebienok**.

The broad slopes, the long southeastern spur, and the compact summit of Slavkovský Štít, soaring to 2452m directly above Starý Smokovec, provide a perfect example of a bird's-eye view. This vista extends from the valley town of Kežmarok in the east to Štrbské Pleso in the west; what's more, standing as it does between the two highest peaks in the High Tatra Mountains (Lomnický Štít and Gerlachovský Štít), Slavkovský also affords spectacular mountain vistas, extending into Poland. The ascent is long certainly, but it's quite straightforward, without any cliffs to climb or chains to grasp. The Shorter walk, to Slavkovská Vyhliadka, a lookout at 1531m, provides particularly good views of Lomnický Štít and the lower reaches of the valleys Vel'ká Studená Dolina and Malá Studená Dolina.

Railway station at Starý Smokovec

Gerlachovský Štít from the summit of Slavkovský Štít

Starting at **Hrebienok**, exit the **funicular station** and turn left with red waymarks, past the hotel and then a ski slope, following a trail into the forest. It's a comparatively easy walk, gaining a little height, to a signposted junction, **Rázcestie pod Slavkovským Štítom (20min)**. Turn right up the blue-waymarked path, through conifers at first, then more varied forest with some birch, and on through dwarf pines — to the first taste of the views to come (**45min**). Suddenly Lomnický Štít appears ahead, and you reach the lookout, **Slavkovská Vyhliadka** (**47min**). *(The Shorter walk returns from here).*

There are even better views further on (**1h2min**) and when you reach the **crest of the spur** (**1h13min**), from where the bright green roof of Zamkovského Chata (Walks 15 and 17) can be seen in the trees far below. The path rises across boulder fields; the skilful use of flat boulders to build flights of steps makes progress surprisingly easy (or at least not difficult!). A few steps beyond another good view of Lomnický Štít (**1h34min**) the route crosses a smallish sloping granite slab, well endowed with natural footholds. Then the path regains the crest (**1h39min**) and traverses a narrow section along the right-hand side of the spur. Beyond a small gap, the path continues to the left, fairly easily and ever upwards, past another small **saddle** (**1h57min**). There follows a series of sharp bends across boulder fields on the western flank, and a brief stretch along the rim of the spur (**2h18min**). The path then leads along the northeastern side for a short distance and up the mountainside, soon zigzagging to traverse the rocks of the summit massif. It winds steeply up to the crest momentarily (the only section lacking well made steps), then goes easily up to the summit of **Slavkovský Štít (3h)**.

The return is merely a matter of retracing your steps, although it seems like a different walk altogether, with your outlook directed almost constantly to the lower slopes and the broad sweep of the valley below. Back at the **lookout (5h2min)**, allow another 20 minutes or more to the signposted **junction (5h25min)** and a similar stretch back to **Hrebienok (5h45min)**.

Walk 17 (Slovakian High Tatras): SKALNATÉ PLESO AND LOMNICKÉ SEDLO

See map on pages 86-87; see also photos on pages 14, 88
Distance: 7km/4.3mi; 2h10min
Grade: moderate (approximately 595m/1950ft ascent); on signposted and waymarked trails and paths
Equipment: see page 31
Refreshments: available at Hrebienok, Skalnatá Chata, Skalnaté Pleso and Tatranská Lomnica
Transport: as Walk 15, page 84, to Hrebienok. Return by chair lift from Lomnické Sedlo to Skalnaté Pleso, then by cable car from Skalnaté Pleso to Tatranská Lomnica, from where you can take a or to Starý Smokovec (see Transport, page 134).
Nearest accommodation: Starý Smokovec, Hrebienok, Tatranská Lomnica
Short walk: Vel'ká Lomnická Veža. 1.4km/0.9mi; 25min. Easy (115m/377ft ascent). Equipment and refreshments as for the main walk (except Hrebienok). Transport: , or to Tatranská Lomnica, then cable car to Skalnaté Pleso (ample parking at the cable car station; see **plan** on reverse of the touring map). Join the main walk at the 1h40min-point, taking the chair lift from Skalnaté Pleso to Lomnické Sedlo. Return the same way. (See Transport, page 134).

Lomnický Štít (2634m; photograph page 14) is the most striking of the peaks above the central High Tatras villages. The second highest Tatra summit, its towering triangle of precipitous cliffs is flanked by equally rugged satellite peaks. It is, of course, unattainable by ordinary mortals on foot, but a chair lift from Skalnaté Pleso at the foot of the cliffs lands you close to an easily negotiable section of the peak's long southeastern spur. From here you can peer down into Malá Studená Dolina and pick out Téryho Chata (Walk 15) near a cluster of tarns. The main walk from Hrebienok above Starý Smokovec reaches Skalnaté Pleso via a very scenic, well graded path; the Short walk takes advantage of the cable car from Tatranská Lomnica to Skalnaté Pleso.

Start the walk to the right of the hotel opposite the **Hrebienok funicular station** beside a 'tree' of signposts. Follow the red route, a broad trail, into the forest. Pass a signposted junction on the right (**14min**); descend through an intersection called **Rázcestie nad Rainerovou Chatou**, and walk down past another junction on the right (**18min**). Beyond a wide bridge, the trail climbs steadily past an impressive waterfall, **Obrovský Vodopád** (**24min**), and emerges into more open dwarf pine woodland with superb views from a sharp left bend (**33min**). Back in tall forest, it's only a few minutes to a path junction (**48min**). Continue straight on (red waymarks), rising steadily, to **Lomnická Vyhliadka** (**1h**), a spectacular viewpoint from where you can see Lomnický Štít and Slavkovský Štít watching over the twin valleys, Vel'ká Studená Dolina and Malá Studená Dolina. The path continues its steady uphill course through birch and dwarf pines, soon affording fine all-round views of the plains below and the low hills scattered around its perimeter. Pass a path junction on the right and soon

19 November 2004

On 19 November 2004 a violent storm tore through the High Tatras. It lasted for about four hours and flattened 250,000ha (9650 acres) of the forest covering the foothills. Winds reached 118km/hour in the towns and up to 194km/hour at Skalnaté Pleso above Tatranská Lomnica. The damage was confined to a fairly narrow swathe generally up to 1100m, from near Podbanské (west of Štrbské Pleso) east to near Tatranská Kotlina. Miraculously only two people were killed, but many buildings were damaged, and roads, railways and paths blocked.

By 2006 all major roads, the railways and many of the paths into the mountains had been reopened. The remaining paths may eventually be cleared; more information should be available from the park offices in Štrbské Pleso and Tatranská Lomnica. The daunting task of clearing the fallen trees was still underway at time of writing, with lorries loaded with logs busy from dawn to dusk. It may well still be in progress when you use this book. For the time being, the areas surrounding Štrbské Pleso, Starý Smokovec and Tatranská Lomnica look rather stark, but there are pockets of miraculously untouched forest and strong signs of natural regeneration. With luck, new forests will steadily develop, and 2004's *kalamity* (as it's known locally) will become a distant memory.

Photograph: sculpture at the national park entrance near Tatranská Lomnica

you reach **Skalnatá Chata** (**1h38min**), a small homely place with a superb outlook and small Slovak-only memu (open from 11am). It's only two minutes more to the rather incongruous **cable car station and restaurant** — all too close to small **Skalnaté Pleso** (**1h40min**). *The Short walk joins here.)*

The lower **Lomnické Sedlo chair lift station** is less than 100m up to the left. From its top station, close to the base of the Lomnický Štít cliffs, follow a fairly steep, green-waymarked path up to the pass itself. The path along the narrow crest of the spur winds around clusters of boulders, near the western rim in places, to the rather amorphous high point of **Vel'ká Lomnická Veža** (**1h55min**; Picnic 11). Vantage points for the awesome views into Malá Studená Dolina and beyond are plentiful. Retrace steps to the top **chair lift station** (**2h10min**), take the chair lift down to **Skalnaté Pleso**, and then take the **cable car** down to **Tatranská Lomnica**.

Walk 18 (Slovakian High Tatras): TWO LAKES AND TWO MOUNTAIN INNS

Distance: 19.2km/12mi; 5h20min
Grade: moderate-strenuous (approximately 900m/2950ft ascent); on signposted and waymarked unsurfaced roads, tracks, trails and paths
Equipment: see page 31
Refreshments: available at Tatranská Kotlina, Chata Plesnivec and Chata pri Zelenom Plese. Water bottles can be replenished where shown on the map (use purifying tablets).
Transport: 🚗 (Car tours 2 and 3), 🚆 or 🚌 to Starý Smokovec or Tatranská Lomnica (see page 72), then 🚌 to Tatranská Kotlina (alight at the 'Carda' bus stop). Return on 🚌 from the 'Biela Voda' stop (see Transport, page 134).
Nearest accommodation: Tatranská Kotlina, Tatranská Lomnica, Starý Smokovec
Shorter walks
1 Chata Plesnivec. 10.2km/6.3mi; 2h45min. Easy-moderate (530m/1740ft ascent). Equipment: see page 31; refreshments at Tatranská Kotlina and Chata Plesnivec. Transport: 🚌 (as for main walk) or 🚗: Tatranská Kotlina is on route 67 (Poprad/Kežmarok/Łysa Polana road), 1.5km northwest of the junction with route 537, the main High Tatras road. There is a car park (fee) in the centre of the village, 0.75km northwest of the start of the walk. From the car park follow a footpath parallel with the road to the starting point. Follow the main walk to **Chata Plesnivec** (1h32min-point). At the signposted junction immediately to the left of the *chata,* turn left down a yellow-waymarked route towards *Čierna Voda*. The track descends quite steeply and rounds a bend, soon passing very close to a stream (**1h42min**). Further on it leads into tall forest (**1h49min**), runs through a small meadow with a picnic table (**1h57min**), then crosses several bridges. At a junction called **Rázcestie Čierna Voda** (**2h17min**), turn left along a track (blue waymarks). Climb slightly and turn right at another junction (**2h22min**), then turn left at a fork. Go on to another junction, **Rázcestie Šumivý Prameň** (**2h25min**), passed earlier in the day. Turn right, then turn right at the next intersection (**2h29min**). With a house in sight, bear right, down a trail (**2h39min**), and continue to an unsurfaced road. Turn right, to return to the start of the walk at **Tatranská Kotlina** (**2h45min**).
2 Vel'ké Biele Pleso. 16.1km/10mi; 4h45min. Moderate (850m/2790ft ascent). Equipment and refreshments as for Shorter walk 1; transport as for the main walk. Follow the main walk to **Vel'ké Biele Pleso** (2h57min-point), then continue south on the blue-waymarked path, following **Walk 19** from the 2h37min-point (page 97) to the **'Biela Voda' bus stop** on the main High Tatras road, northeast of Tatranská Lomnica.

The Belianske Tatry region adjoining the central High Tatras to the northeast, is strikingly different from its western neighbour, with its narrow ridges and precipitous peaks. The Belianske mountains are more gracefully contoured, with characteristic long lines of limestone cliffs in the uppermost reaches. The valleys are wider, and the area is less frequented than the sometimes-crowded High Tatras. The two lakes visited during this exceptionally scenic walk dra-

Vel'ké Biele Pleso

matically portray the contrasts between the two regions: the pastoral setting of Vel'ké Biele Pleso and the spectacularly rugged surroundings of Zelené Pleso. The first Shorter walk provides a good introduction to the area, and the second an appreciation of the contrasts described.

You start at the **'Carda' bus stop** on the southeastern edge of **Tatranská Kotlina**, where a clutch of **national park signs** points along a minor road. Following blue and green waymarks, walk along the road and, at a signposted junction after a minute, turn left along an unsurfaced road. In another minute turn left again, along a trail which leads up to a track; turn left once more. Pass a small **water supply building** on the right (**9min**), beyond which the track climbs quite steeply. Ten minutes later (**19min**), turn left along a trail and cross a small stream.

You rise to a junction, **Rázcestie Šumivý Prameň** (**27min**). Bear right with green waymarks along a track, climbing steeply. In autumn the sycamores in the surrounding forest glow bright yellow. Leave the track at the first distinct bend, by turning sharp left turn along a path (waymarked just beyond the turn; **35min**). Soon the path enters conifer forest, crosses a spur, then traverses steadily up **Dolina Siedmich Prameňov**. The towering peak of Lomnický Štít makes its first appearance through a gap in the trees (**47min**) and, half an hour later, the *chata* appears (**1h26min**). A final steep haul brings you to the balcony of **Chata Plesnivec** (**1h32min**), with an all-Slovak menu at time of writing. A plaque on the western wall commemorates a visit in 1813 by the internationally renowned Swedish botanist, Goran Wahlenberg; he must have travelled quite widely — two tarns in Furkotská Dolina above Štrbské Pleso are named after him (Walk 12). *(Shorter walk 1 leaves the main walk at this point.)*

Continue steeply up the green-waymarked path towards *Biele Pleso,* within a few minutes crossing a small stream from where there's a fine panoramic view of the crescent of cliffs and

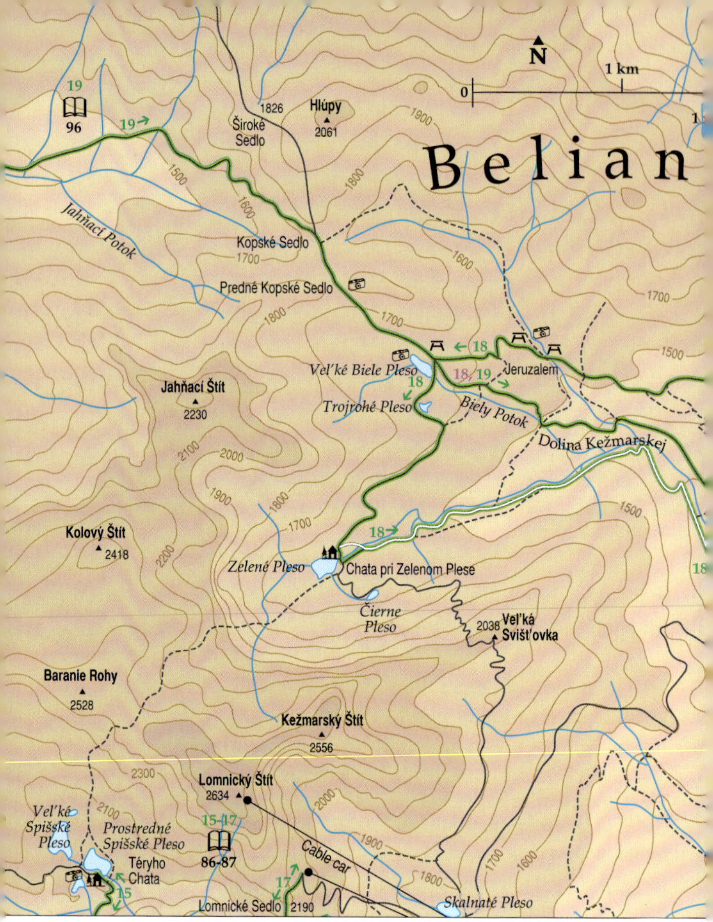

slender grassy slopes above the *chata*. The path leads up through conifer forest, across a few small pockets of fallen trees and another small stream (**1h57min**) from where the gradient eases. Soon dwarf pines appear, and the path leads into a beautiful meadow (**2h6min**). Follow a trail through scattered conifers, then a path, to reach a superbly sited **picnic table** (**2h33min**) in a small clearing, with a magnificent view of Lomnický Štít. Two minutes later you're at **Jeruzalem**, a graceful expanse of grassland, clumps of dwarf pines and scattered mountain ash trees. The path soon begins to rise, past another **picnic table** (**2h43min**) and on to a full-scale picnic area just above **Veľké Biele Pleso** (**2h57min**). *(Shorter walk 2 leaves us here.)*

Continue south on the red-waymarked path to the right, crossing the lake's outlet on a **footbridge**. You go through dwarf pines, past grass-fringed **Trojrohé Pleso** (**3h2min**), across a spur and into a completely different valley landscape: steep, towering peaks, all rock and no grass. The path descends steeply, then traverses to the spectacularly sited **Chata pri Zelenom Plese** (**3h37min**) beside the beautiful lake, **Zelené Pleso**. The Slovak-only menu has helpful illustrations!

From here descend steps, cross

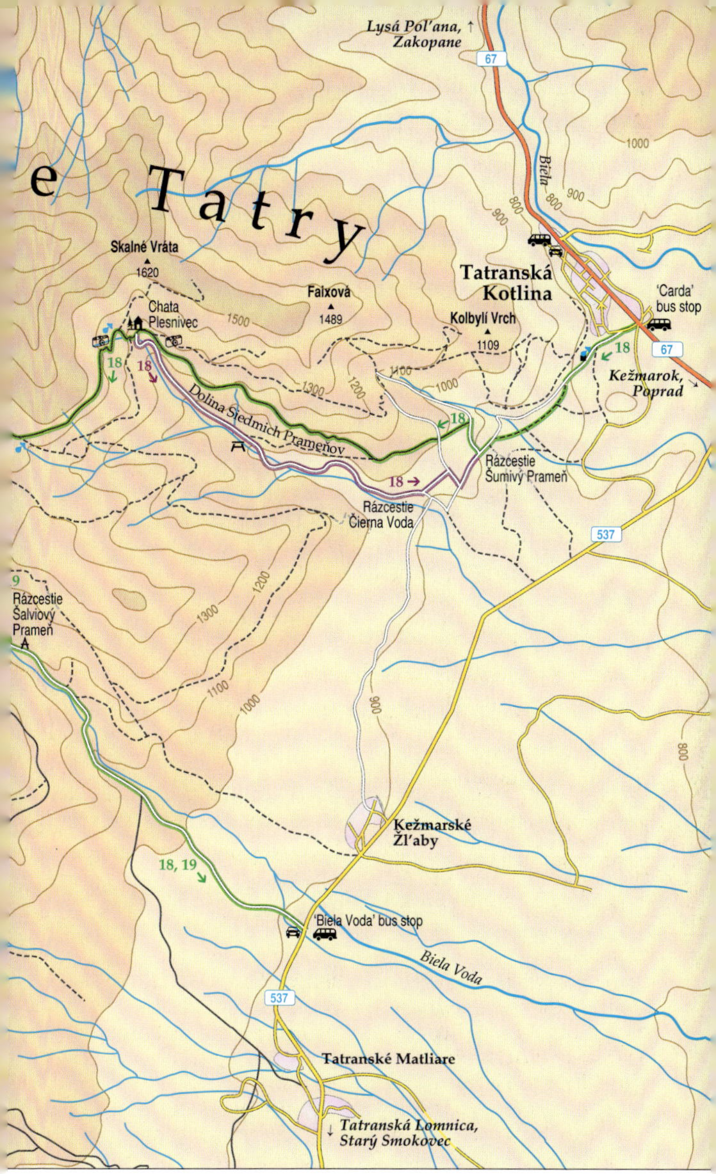

the lake's outlet stream, and turn left on a trail (yellow waymarks). You soon join a wide rocky track. It descends steadily into conifers, becoming less stony after the second sharp bend (**4h19min**). Continue down past a path junction on the right (**4h33min**; picnic shelter) and then a track junction on the right. Cross a bridge to a major junction, **Rázcestie Salviový Prameň** (**4h40min**). The unsurfaced road from here provides blissfully easy walking, shortly passing another picnic shelter. Descending steadily, you reach storm-damaged forest (**5h16min**) not far from the **'Biela Voda' bus stop/parking area** on the main road (**5h20min**).

Walk 19 (Slovakian High Tatras): FROM TATRANSKÁ JAVORINA TO BIELA VODA

Map ends on pages 94-95
Distance: 16.7km/10.4mi; 4h23min
Grade: moderate (approximately 760m/2500ft ascent); on signposted and waymarked minor road, unsurfaced roads, tracks, trails and paths
Equipment: see page 31
Refreshments: only available at Tatranská Javorina
Transport: 🚌 to Tatranská Javorina and back from Biela Voda (see Transport, page 134). Travelling by car, park at the Biela Voda bus stop, then take a 🚌 to Tatranská Javorina to start.
Nearest accommodation: Tatranská Kotlina, Tatranská Lomnica, Starý Smokovec
Short walk: Pod Muráňom
4.2km/2.6mi; 56min. Easy (80m/260ft ascent). Equipment and refreshments as for the main walk. Transport: 🚌 (as for the main walk) or 🚗 (Car tour 2) to and from Tatranská Javorina. There is limited parking space opposite the shop in this small village. Follow the main walk to the 28min-point, an attractive meadow with picnic tables; retrace steps from there.

More so than circular walks, linear walks are, I think, more satisfying — starting quite far perhaps from your base, traversing valleys and passes to reach a point closer to home and transport. The Belianske Tatra region, northeast of the central High Tatras, is ideal for such a cross-country walk, with long, rarely steep valleys, and comparatively broad passes. This walk starts close to the Polish border at Tatranská Javorina and follows a southeasterly route up the beautiful valley of Zadné Med'odoly and down the quite different Dolina Kezmarsky to Biela Voda on the High Tatras road.

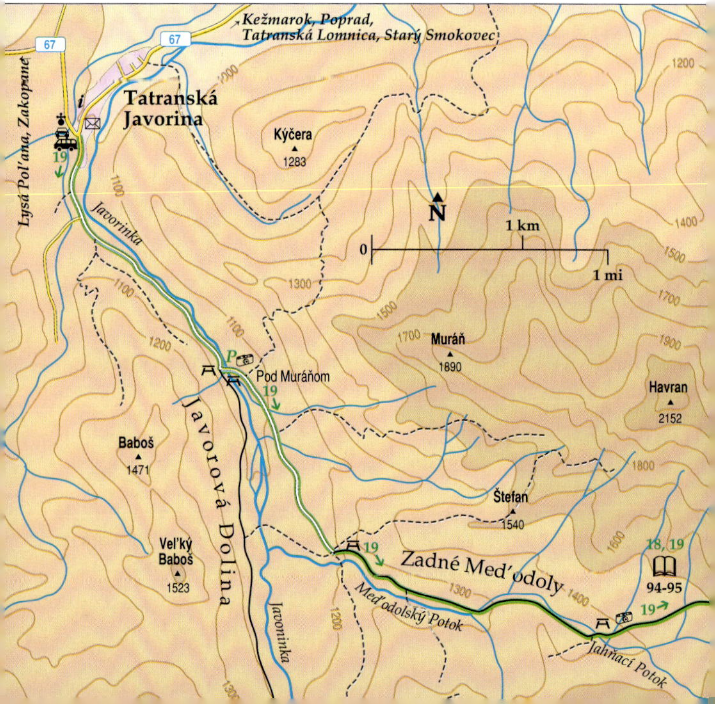

Landscape mid-way along the Zadné Med'odoly Valley

Start in **Tatranská Javorina**: follow the minor road opposite the **shop** (near a sharp bend in the main road). Beyond some **national park signposts** and an information board the road is unsurfaced and starts to gain height through varied forest. It leads to a junction beside a bridge and a picnic shelter at a place called **Pod Muráňom (28min)**, dramatically overlooked by the sheer western face of Muran's huge bluff. *(The Short walk and Picnic 12 retrace steps from here.)*

There are more picnic tables near the **wooden house** just across the bridge, on the edge of the beautiful meadow. Continue across the grass, up into conifer forest. The unsurfaced road becomes a trail, bending left at a minor junction (**43min**) with another picnic table. The trail climbs steeply, soon penetrating a small, rather deep canyon, and goes on through the forest to a **bridge** (**1h3min**). It crosses another **bridge (1h13min)**, where there are more picnic tables on the far side. By now you are in the middle reaches of the valley, **Zadné Med'odoly**, and in two minutes you come to another, most attractive meadow from where the view embraces spiky peaks along a crest to the south and grassy, pine-clad slopes and elongated limestone cliffs to the north. Now you're on a path, climbing fairly steeply through two small copses of conifers; it eventually leads into grassland (**1h45min**) and on to a saddle, **Kopské Sedlo (2h 10min)**, where you keep ahead at the signposted junction.

In just five minutes you reach another saddle, **Predné Kopské Sedlo**, with a good view of the wide plains to the east. From here the path winds steeply down through dwarf pines to the shore of **Vel'ké Biele Pleso (2h37min)** and the adjacent picnic area, a popular place on weekends. From the signposted path junction, follow the blue-waymarked route, mostly rocky, down into **Dolina Kežmarskej**. Beyond a footbridge the path leads into conifers (**2h55min**) and descends steadily, across bridges, through mixed forest, past a picnic shelter (**3h25min**) and on to a junction, **Rázcestie Salviový Prameň** (**3h43min**). From here descend the unsurfaced road, passing a picnic shelter, to the **bus stop/car park** at **Biela Voda (4h23min)** on the main High Tatras road.

SLOVENSKÝ RAJ NATIONAL PARK

Slovenský Raj National Park (Slovak Paradise; Walks 20-22) is alone among the six parks featured in this guide in not being predominantly mountainous in character, although there are several high points above 1000m. The key features of this 19,763ha/48,800 acre park, proclaimed in 1988, derive from its characteristic limestone — a network of deep, narrow gorges and approximately 350 caves.

Coniferous forests cover most of the ridges and spurs, and the park is especially important for the protection of a wide array of wildlife, from bears to butterflies, including many endemic species. The 16km-long canyon of the river Hornád *(Prielom Hornádu)* in the north of the park is the longest; it and several other shorter, but much steeper canyons have been made accessible by the installation of metal steps (*stúpačky;* see photograph), ladders, bridges and chains. The Kláštorisko Plateau, immediately south of the Hornád Valley and protected by gorges on three sides, has been inhabited for centuries; a visit to the remains of the 14th-century monastery there is featured in Walk 22 (page 105).

The private website www.slovenskyraj.sk has some information about the park in English, and links to sites offering local accommodation.

The nearest transport hub is the town of Spišská Nová Ves, on the main train line between Košice (Slovakia's second city) and Poprad (Slovakian High Tatras), Liptovský Mikuláš (Low Tatras), Žilina (Malá Fatra) and Bratislava, with daily departures at least hourly, more frequently between 10.00 and early evening. Some services continue to Prague in the Czech Republic. Daily long-distance and regional bus services operate to the same destinations. For Poprad there are four departures plus another three Mon-Fri.

SAD operates a bus service from Spišská Nová Ves to Čingov, a small settlement about 24km/15mi southeast of Poprad, which provides a pleasant base for walks in the park. There are three departures Mon-Fri, two Sat-Sun, and four more departures in the afternoon and evening in high season. From Čingov there's a daily service to Spišská Nová Ves at 08.45 (and three more much later, but only from 15/6-31/8). There are three more departures Mon-Fri and one Sat-Sun. See transport details for Walks 20-22 on page 134.

Walk 20 (Slovenský Raj): HORNÁD GORGE AND TOMÁŠOVSKÝ VÝHĽAD

See map on page 102; see photograph page 16
Distance: 12km/7.4mi; 4h6min
Grade: moderate (approximately 200m/650ft ascent); on signposted and waymarked tracks, trails and paths, *but you must be sure-footed and have a head for heights (see the introduction below)*
Equipment: see page 31
Refreshments: available at Čingov and possibly at Pri Letanovskom Mlyne
Transport: 🚗 (Car tour 4) or 🚂 and then 🚌 to Čingov (see page 98 and Transport, page 134). Motorists: park at Čingov just inside the national park entrance; pay the parking and entrance fees at the gate.

Nearest accommodation: Čingov
Shorter walk: Tomášovský Výhľad. 7.7km/4.8mi; 1h51min. Easy-moderate (approximately 200m/650ft ascent). Equipment and transport as for the main walk; refreshments only at Čingov Parkovisko. This walk provides an introduction to the **Hornád Gorge**, but leaves it before the first of the ladders and steps which enable the full-length traverse. Follow the main walk to the path junction at the 1h3min-point. Turn right up the green-waymarked path; it climbs steeply to a junction (no signpost); turn right with yellow waymarks, rejoining the main walk at the 3h12min-point and follow it to the end.

The Hornád Gorge (Prielom Hornádu) is undoubtedly the highlight of Slovenský Raj National Park; it's probably the most popular walk in the park and has been so for more than 30 years. Its undoubted challenges necessarily involve climbing and descending wooden ladders, crossing rock outcrops with the help of chain handrails or steps cut into the rock and/or firmly secured metal rungs and steps, and walking along short metal bridges with chain handrails. You'll also traverse series of metal grids (approximately 35cm x 70cm) on struts securely bolted to the limestone cliffs from which they extend, and several metres above the river or its bank, with chain handrails along the cliff face (see photograph opposite). Neither special skills nor equipment are required to negotiate these fixtures, but they may be unnerving if you suffer from vertigo. Nevertheless, I do believe that almost everyone should be able to enjoy this extraordinary walk.

It is possible to go right through the gorge in a few hours, but there's much to be said for exploring it on two circular walks, from each end, to enjoy views of the gorge and the surrounding deep valleys and high ridges to the south. Accordingly, this walk includes a justifiably popular lookout directly above the lowermost reaches of the gorge. The Shorter walk offers a glimpse of typical limestone cliffs and the tumbling stream, without any ladders.

Warning If you spot an alternative route back to Čingov from the Trstený Potok junction beyond Letanovský Mlyn, via the road towards Letanovce, a track to Spišské Tomášovce and roads from there, then think again! We followed this route and, shortly beyond the edge of the forest, passed an untidy settlement. From here we were shadowed by children, youths and young men pestering us for money; they persisted until we turned off the road along a field track. It was an unnerving experience, to be avoided at all costs.

Starting at the southern end of the **car park** at **Čingov** (just past the **bus stop** on the right), bear right along a minor road with blue and yellow waymarks. This leads to a smaller parking area, a picnic site and an intersection (**10min**). Continue straight ahead along the unsurfaced road; bear left at a junction (**13min**) and two minutes later, pass an **information board** outlining the main features of the gorge. Soon, cross a bridge and continue along a trail. Bear right at a junction (**15min**). The trail undulates somewhat through varied forest to another junction, **Biely Potok Ústie** (**51min**).

Following blue waymarks, cross the nearby **bridge** and turn right along a path. Climb up a rock outcrop (with chain handrail) and,

Lanová Lavka suspension bridge over the Hornád (Walk 21)

at a path junction, bear right with green waymarks (**56min**).

Beyond a bridge, you pass a junction on the right (**1h3min**). *(The Shorter walk turns right here.)*

The valley narrows markedly as you reach the next feature, **Mostík nad Úžinou** (**1h31min**), where a couple of chains help you cross a bluff. Then you come to **Stúpačky nad Tišinou** — wide metal grids across the cliff face; these lead to a wooden ladder and a few more metal grids. Next is the similar but longer **Stúpačky pri Jaskyni**, soon followed by more of the same at **Stúpačky pod Mlynom** — descending and level metal grids beside the cliff face (photograph page 98). And that's it — the rest is conventional walking!

A short stretch through forest leads to a wooden footbridge beyond which a level trail continues through the forest (**2h9min**). At **Letanovský Mlyn**, a path junction, go straight ahead with blue waymarks, across a wide bridge, **Kartiziansky Most**, to another junction, where you turn right towards *Čingov* (**2h13min**). Before doing so however, you could bear left and continue to a small grassy clearing and the possibility of refreshments and certainly picnic tables at **Pri Letanovskom Mlyne** (**2h18min**).

Return to the junction and turn left towards *Čingov* (**2h23min**). Walk along the track to an unsignposted junction on the right, almost opposite a **cabin** in the trees on the left (**2h30min**). Climb staight uphill on a path for about a minute, then turn sharp right at a fork along a trail. Continue steadily up, across a wide, shallow valley, to the rim of the ridge and a good **viewpoint** (**2h33min**). The trail soon levels out and becomes a track through tall forest. Shortly, keep left at a junction; descend slightly, then bear right at a minor junction along a track (**2h44min**).

Soon you have a view of villages and small towns in the valley to the north. Stay on the main track, keeping left if in doubt, until you reach open ground at the top of a field (**2h55min**). At a signposted intersection at a place called **Pri Tomáš Výhľade** (**3h7min**), turn right along a track (yellow waymarks) leading into the forest. Ignore an unwaymarked track and climb to a junction near low cliffs on the left (**3h12min**). *(The Shorter walk rejoins here.)*

Turn sharp left uphill with green and yellow waymarks, go through a small cleft, and bear left to pass a low crag. You climb gradually to the magnificent lookout, **Tomášovský Výhľad** (**3h18min**) — a broad, flat balcony dropping sheer to the valley below with views almost the full length of the canyon.

From the signposted junction continue on a path with yellow waymarks towards *Čingov,* soon passing another good viewpoint. Further on, at a minor junction where there's another lookout to the right (**3h30min**), continue to the left, gently downhill. The path bends left, widens to a trail and soon becomes a track; it descends to an unsurfaced road. Turn right beside a derelict restaurant (**3h 44min**). Follow the track between fields, with small wooden cottages on the right, to a junction in front of the office of **Autokamping Tatran**. Turn right and walk down the field, past chalets on the left, to a trail leading into the forest. At a junction near some houses, turn right along a path and go down dissected rocks and steps to a road. Turn left to the **car park** and **bus stop** at **Čingov** (**4h6min**).

Hrabušice →
Letanovce ↗
N
0
1 km
1 mi
Podlesok
Hrdlo Hornádu
Veľká Biela Voda
Zelená Hora
654
Čertova Sihoť
638
Kláštorská Roklina
Pri Letanovskom Mlyne
Trstený Potok
Letanovský Mlyn
Pri Tomáš Výhľade
Tomášovský Výhľad
Hornád
Hadušovce
Spišské Tomášovce
Smižany
536
Spišská Nová Ves
Maša
Čingov
Park
Autokamping Tatran
Rumanová
927
Kláštorisko
838
Kláštorisko Chata
Kláštorisko Lúka
Biely Potok Rázcestie
Biely Potok Ústie
Biely Potok
Kyseľ Ústie
Prielom Hornádu
652

Walk 21 (Slovenský Raj): HORNÁD GORGE (WESTERN END)

See map opposite; see also photograph page 100
Distance: 10.5km/6.5mi; 4h30min
Grade: moderate (approximately 200m/650ft ascent); on signposted and waymarked paths, trails and tracks, *but you must be sure-footed and have a head for heights* (see introduction to Walk 20, page 99, for details of traversing the gorge)
Equipment: see page 31
Refreshments: available at Podlesok and perhaps at Pri Letanovskom Mlyne
Transport: 🚗 (near Car tour 4) or 🚆 and then 🚌 to Podlesok, or 🚌 from Spišská Nová Ves via Hrabušice to Podlesok (see page 98 and Transport, page 134). Travelling by car, from Čingov follow the road to Spišská Nová Ves and, at a junction beside a railway underpass (1.8km) continue ahead under the railway and go on to a junction with the main road, route 536 (2.3km). Follow this northwest to a junction in the town of Spišský Štvrtok (8.6km). Turn left and follow a minor road through countryside and the village of Hrabušice (13.2km). Continue past a junction on the right to Betlanovce (14.2km), cross a bridge, and bear left at a junction (15.2km), to drive on to the Podlesok national park entrance (15.5km). Park on the left, just beyond the small office where you pay the entry and parking fee.
Nearest accommodation: Podlesok, Čingov

If the traverse of the eastern end of the renowned Hornád Gorge (Walk 20) has whetted your appetite for this most unusual type of walk, then the western end of the gorge is not to be missed. If anything the western section, described here, is easier or less challenging, and certainly shorter, than the eastern section. Tackling the ladders in the upstream direction seems more natural, so this walk starts near the small settlement of Podlesok and traverses the ridge above the gorge to the north. Please note the warning about beggars along the road which leads northwest out of the national park from the junction at Trstený Potok (see Walk 20, page 99).

Start at **Podlesok** from the **national park entrance gate**: follow the road straight ahead across a bridge, then turn left with blue waymarks across open ground. Beyond a defunct restaurant, the road starts to rise into forest; where it bends slightly to the right (**14min**). Continue straight on along a trail beside the forest, closely following a stream. The path, which could be muddy in places, soon wanders up and down through forest and comes to a short ladder up a low cliff. From the top of the ladder continue across a bridge to an intersection called **Hrdlo Hornádu**, with a small **shelter**, where a park officer may ask to see your entry ticket (**28min**; Picnic 13). Following yellow waymarks, climb steeply up the path, across a field, under an old **ski tow** and up along a trail into forest. Tall trees obscure any view from the flat summit of **Zelená Hora** (**49min**). Follow a path which winds down a steep slope to a saddle, then leads on past viewpoints on the right (notably at **1h3min**) and across the edge of a small clearing. From here climb fairly steeply; there's a good view from open

One of the 'innocuous bridges' near Hrdlo Hornádu

ground where a **power line** crosses the gorge (**1h18min**). The path descends slightly, then soon leads along the crest, with good views both to the north and across the gorge. Beyond a short stretch through the forest, there are more excellent vantage points (**1h33min**, **1h39min**) — the best of all being a grassy ledge just past the summit of **Čertova Sihot'** (**1h44min**). Further on the path turns sharp left and descends through patches of nettles to a junction called **Trstený Potok** (**2h10min**); turn right on the track here for a short distance, to an intersection. Again turn right (blue waymarks) and walk past some cottages and on to a small **restaurant** ('Bufet'); if it's closed, there are picnic tables just beside it (**2h15min**).

From the *bufet* follow a trail across open ground to a suspension foot bridge. Cross over and, after about 50m, bear left uphill to negotiate a rocky outcrop via metal steps. These lead to a wooden ladder up a slope, two bridges, and a metal ladder back down to river level. The path soon crosses a tributary (**2h25min**); beyond a wooden bridge there's an easy stretch through forest, leading to a wooden suspension footbridge called **Retažová Lavká nad Zelenou Dolinou**. Then in quick succession you make progress down a flight of steps, go round a bend to a wooden bridge, along a forest path and across a cliff face on metal grids. Another forest path provides a brief respite before you reach **Stúpačky pri Žarese**, metal grids which take you up around a tight bend in the river, across a crag and a series of metal steps. This is followed by a similar succession of forest paths and ladders, to the long suspension bridge shown on page 100, **Lanová Lavka**, then a path junction, **Kláštorská Roklina** (**3h**), with an interesting information board.

Almost immediately you cross the cliff face on a line of metal steps, a couple of which are directly above the river. Continue through forest to a flight of wooden ladders (**3h10min**) which land you at the start of **Stúpačky nad Večným Daždom**, another of the now-familiar combination of metal grids and bridges. The path then crosses a tributary and leads on through forest to a bridge, **Retazový Most** (**3h22min**).

On the far side a forest path leads to **Stúpačky pri Mníchovej Diere** (**3h30min**), where some of the metal grids are suspended above the river. A forest path leads on to a short, fairly steep descent down a rocky outcrop (with chain handrail). Then **Stúpačky pod Zelenou Horou**, about 20m long, takes you mostly above the river (**3h44min**). Back in the forest, a steep ascent on a wooden ladder inevitably leads to a steep descent, partly via rocky steps and metal grids, to river level.

It's plain sailing from here, along a path, past a log cabin and across innocuous bridges, back to **Hrdlo Hornádu** (**4h10min**), the path junction at the ticket checker's shelter. Retrace your steps from here to **Podlesok** (**4h30min**).

Walk 22 (Slovenský Raj): THE HORNÁD RIVER AND HISTORIC KLÁŠTORISKO

See map on page 102
Distance: 14.3km/8.9mi; 4h
Grade: moderate (approximately 400m/1310ft ascent); on sign-posted and waymarked roads, tracks, trails, paths and short wooden footbridges beside low cliffs. A few short sections are equipped with chain handrails.
Equipment: see page 31
Refreshments: available at Čingov and Kláštorisko Chata
Transport: 🚗 (Car tour 4) or 🚂 and then 🚌 to Čingov (see page 98 and Transport, page 134). Motorists: park at Čingov just inside the national park entrance; pay the parking and entrance fees at the gate.
Nearest accommodation: Čingov

Slovenský Raj seems an improbable location for a monastery, but one did flourish here between about 1300 and 1596, high above the gorges, in the shadow of a mountaintop above the middle reaches of the river Hornád. The extensive, partly restored remains — including a church, cloisters, the sacristy and monks' cells — lie just below Kláštorisko Chata, where food and drinks are available (or you can picnic in a secluded spot on the northern side of the monastery site). Add to this the splendid wide views and an attractive stream-side walk, and you have a fine day's outing.

Starting at the southern end of the **car park** at **Čingov** (just past the **bus stop** on the right), bear right along a minor road with blue and yellow waymarks. This leads to a smaller parking area, a picnic site and an intersection (**10min**). Continue straight ahead along the unsurfaced road; bear left at a junction (**13min**) and two minutes later, pass an **information board** outlining the main features of the gorge. Soon, cross a bridge and continue along a trail. Bear right at a junction (**15min**). The trail undulates somewhat through varied forest to another junction, **Biely Potok Ústie** (**51min**).
Turn left along a trail with green waymarks, through varied forest. After a while the trail descends to the stream, **Biely Potok** (**58min**). Some 25 minutes further on you come to a wooden bridge about

Kláštorisko

The 25m-long wooden bridge beside Biely Potok, with chain handholds on the side of the cliff

25m long beside a low cliff and just above water level — it's really quite easy! A path leads onward, gaining some height and crossing a tributary (**1h6min**). Cross Biely Potok on a metal bridge (**1h14min**), then traverse a small bridge across a gap (**1h20min**). Soon, the short length of chain beside a low cliff might be useful (**1h25min**). Continue across a wooden bridge, then beside the stream and over another foot-bridge. Then, just before a third footbridge, turn right up a yellow-waymarked path (**1h31min**). Unhelpfully, the signpost at this junction, called **Kysel' Ústie**, is on the far side of the stream.

It's a steep climb; the chain hand-rails on sections of the dissected sloping limestone crags are there to help you with the climbing, rather than to provide security. The gradient eventually eases slightly (**1h51min**), and the route winds uphill. The next outcrop, of comfortably angled limestone, has what is, rest assured, the *last* chain handrail and two short sets of metal grids or steps, making the climb much easier (**1h53min**). Within a few minutes the path levels out, and you soon come to a signposted junction called **Kláštorisko Lúka** (**2h**), at the edge of a meadow. On a clear day the High Tatras peaks are visible to the northwest.

Turn left with blue waymarks and, shortly, turn left again, to reach a large information board (with English text; **2h10min**) about **Kláštorisko**, just 200m to the north, across the meadow.

Nearby **Kláštorisko Chata** over-looks the monastery site and a sloping meadow dotted with wooden cottages. In the *chata*'s dining room there's an interesting display of artefacts and photos of the site; the menu is in Slovak only.

Return to **Kláštorisko Lúka** (**2h20min**), but continue straight on with blue waymarks towards *Čingov*. The path leads up along the edge of the adjacent forest, meets a trail and rises to a tall **communications tower** on a summit, confusingly also called **Kláštorisko** (**2h26min**).

The descent eventually starts in earnest where there's a glimpse northwards (**2h38min**); the path soon switches to the southern side of the spur and affords an excellent view of the Biely Potok valley. The wide path, soon a trail, keeps close to the rim of the spur for several minutes, then steepens as it drops down the slope (**3h**), soon starting to zigzag. It con-tinues steeply down to a junction, **Biely Potok Rázcestie** (**3h 19min**). Turn right here, go down a rock outcrop (by now the chain handrail should be superfluous!), and cross a bridge. Back at the **Biely Potok Ústie** junction (**3h23min**), you rejoin the outward route. Retrace your steps to **Čingov** (**4h**).

SLOVAKIA'S LOW TATRA NATIONAL PARK

The name 'Low Tatra' is somewhat misleading for this large national park (Walks 23-25). The highest peaks on its broad central, east/west ridge just exceed 2000m, and the 81,000ha/ 200,000 acre park is, in fact, more extensive than the Tatra National Park to the northeast.

The Low Tatra (Nízke Tatry) National Park is the second most visited mountainous area in Slovakia, and the ski resort at Jasná, near the head of the long, deep Demänová Valley, is generally regarded as the best in the country. The resort also serves as a convenient base for walks in the park; waymarked paths and trails traverse ridges, spurs and valleys, and there is a handy chair lift to whisk you high up the slopes all year round.

Beech and conifer forests clothe the lower and middle reaches, with dwarf pines above. The central ridge is dotted with granite tors, and there are some impressive cliffs on the northern face. Granite gives way to limestone midway along the Demänová Valley, where one of the large caves is open for inspection.

The park lies on the southern side of the wide Vah Valley and is readily accessible from the large town of Liptovský Mikuláš, the transport hub for the area. It is on the main train line between Košice (in the east), Spišská Nová Ves (Slovenský Raj), Poprad (Slovakian High Tatras), Žilina (Malá Fatra) and Bratislava — with at least hourly departures. Some services continue to Prague in the Czech Republic. Liptovský Mikuláš is also served by long distance SAD buses between the same centres, and there is a SAD bus service linking Liptovský Mikuláš with Slovakia's High Tatras via Štrbské Pleso and Starý Smokovec, at least twice daily. See transport details for Walks 23-25 on page 134.

Photograph: junipers, ubiquitous in the Tatras

Walk 23 (Low Tatras): TWO VALLEYS ABOVE JASNÁ

Distance: 14km/8.7mi; 4h52min
Grade: moderate (approximately 725m/2380ft ascent); on sign-posted and waymarked tracks, trails and paths
Equipment: see page 31
Refreshments: available in Jasná. Water is available at stream crossings as marked on the map (use purifying tablets).
Transport: 🚗 (Car tour 5) or 🚆 and then 🚌 to the Demänová Valley and on to Jasná (see page 107 and Transport, page 134). Return by bus from a stop near Chata Lúčky. Motorists: there is a large car park in Jasná below the Hotel Grand, adjacent to the bus terminus; you can also park a short way above the end of the walk, opposite the entrance to Chata Lúčky.
Nearest accommodation: Jasná, Demänová Valley
Shorter walk: Jasná viewpoint. 8.5km/5.3mi; 3h3min. Easy-moderate (approximately 450m/1475ft ascent). Equipment, refreshments and transport as for the main walk. Follow the main walk to the 1h54min-point for fine **views over Jasná**. Return to the **Pod Orlou Skalou** junction (the 1h46min-point) and turn left on a blue-waymarked path down through conifer forest. Cross a **ski run**; turn left down the eastern edge of the open ground for about 200m, then recross the run, to go back into forest. Descend a path past a derelict building, across the edge of the Hotel Liptov car park, to a minor road. Turn right, down to a wider road; the **bus stop/car park** are some 400m to the right.

High Tatras from near Luková

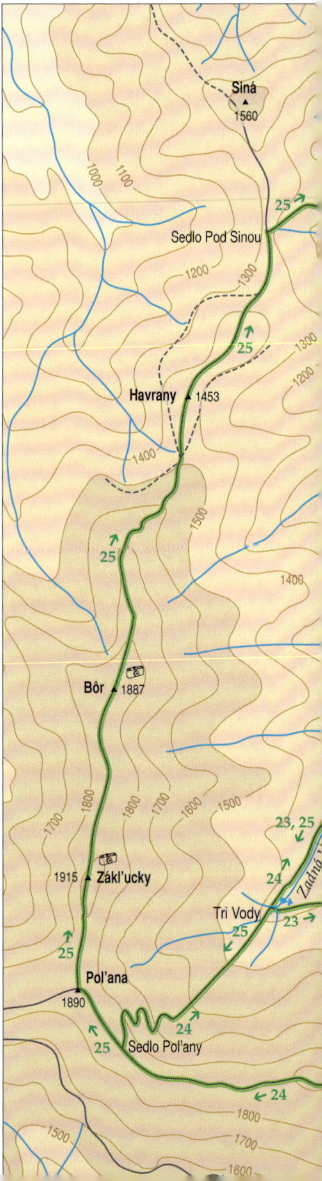

This walk takes you up to and across the middle reaches of the long east/west ridge in the heart of the Low Tatras (Nízke Tatry) National Park, and offers a good introduction to the geography and scenery of the area. The route follows a nature trail, complete with several information boards describing everything from the local geology to the activities of the partisans here during the later stages of World War II; the text is in Slovak, but the illustrations are sufficiently graphic to give you some idea of the messages.

Start from the **bus terminus** at **Jasná**, below the Hotel Grand: go up a path past the hotel and turn right along a road. Follow this around a bend and on to **Mikulášska Chata** on the right (**10min**). Turn left along a road (yellow waymarks), soon passing a hotel on the left. From an official-looking building (also on the left; **19min**) take a trail into conifer forest. Keep left at a junction (**23min**). Further on, bear right (**32min**) across two log bridges. Climbing gradually, you reach an **information board** (**38min**) and continue up a well-made path beside the stream, **Zadná Voda**, to **Tri Vody** (**58min**), the confluence of three streams. Cross two of the streams on flat boulders and climb steps to a signposted junction; turn left (red waymarks). The path undulates but generally gains height. You cross a log bridge (**1h4min**) and later a stream, and come to a **notice board** about the Skalka National Nature Reserve (**1h24min**), with a good view of a long high spur to the west. A little higher, at a place called **Brhliská** at the top of a ski lift, the outlook is even more extensive (**1h29min**). The path then goes under another lift, across a stream and on to a signposted junction, **Pod Orlou Skalou** (**1h46min**). Continuing with both red and blue markers, you're soon among dwarf pines, following an excellent path up a steep slope, past a fine **viewpoint** above Jasná (**1h 54min**). *(The Shorter walk returns from here.)*

At a **chair lift station**, bear left along a track, then go right up steps to a signposted path junction, **Luková** (**2h16min**), almost beneath a defunct chair lift. Bear left downhill (red waymarks), past the top of another chair lift, to a broad stone-paved path. Here you're high above the Demänová Valley, with views to local peaks and the lowlands to the north — including the broad expanses of Liptovská Mara (a lake). Pass under a chair lift and go on to the top station of another lift, where you follow the sign for *Široká Dolina* (**2h36min**). Continue down the grassy slope on a track of sorts; follow it round a right-hand bend and down through a wide clearing in conifer forest to a place called **Pekná Vyhliadka** (**2h51min**), at the base of a ski lift that is partly hidden in trees. Continue down a path through the forest; it crosses a footbridge (**2h56min**), then a smaller stream, and climbs past a **notice board**. It then goes through a small open area with a good view of the precipitous rock- and tree-clad mountainside above (**3h8min**). The paved path leads on over a low spur and down to the **Luková stream**, which you cross on huge flat boulders (**3h14min**). Then go up and over another spur to a signposted path junction in the valley **Široká Dolina** (**3h26min**), next to an **information board** about iron ore mining.

The path from here is *very* stony; walkers have created 'bypasses'. You descend past another **notice board** (**3h48min**), to a **footbridge** (**4h7min**) and then a junction, **Pod Krčahovom** (**4h 27min**). **Board 11** (**4h39min**) explains the Slovak partisans' activities in the area. Continue down into a meadow with very few waymarks: go directly down the gentle slope towards some **wooden buildings**. About 30m to the right is a fenced enclosure with a **grave** (**4h46min**), seemingly dating from 1945. Continue past a last information board, opposite a memorial plaque, and on to the valley road and the **bus stop** near **Chata Lúčky** (**4h52min**).

Walk 24 (Low Tatras): THE ASCENT OF CHOPOK AND A FINE RIDGE WALK

See map on pages 108-109
Distance: 15.2km/9.4mi; 5h
Grade: strenuous (approximately 970m/3180ft ascent); on signposted and waymarked tracks, trails and paths
Equipment: see page 31
Refreshments: available at Mikulášska Chata and Kamenná Chata near Chopok. Water bottles can be replenished at Tri Vody (use purifying tablets).
Transport: (Car tour 5) or and then to the Demänová Valley and on to Jasná (see page 107 and Transport, page 134). Motorists: there is a large parking area below the Hotel Grand, adjacent to the bus terminus.
Nearest accommodation: Jasná
Shorter walks
1 Chopok by chair lift. 2km/1.2mi; 1h. Easy (approximately 364m/1190ft ascent). Equipment: see page 31; refreshments available at Kamenná Chata. Transport: or to Záhradky. By car, park beside the main road, opposite the access road to the chair lift to Chopok Úboč. Travelling by public transport, either walk down the main road from Jasná to Záhradky or take a bus (see Transport, page 134). Take the chair lift to Chopok Úboč and join the main walk at 1h52min-point, to reach the summit of Chopok then Kamenná Chata. Retrace steps back to the upper lift station.
2 Chopok and the ridge. 8.6km/5.3mi; 3h. Moderate (approximately 420m/1380ft ascent). Equipment and refreshments as for the main walk; transport as *Shorter walk 1*. Join main walk at 1h52min-point, at the top of the chair lift, and follow it to the end. Return the 1km to Záhradky (if you left a car there) on foot or by bus (see Transport, page 134).

Chopok (2024m) may not be quite the highest summit in the Low Tatras National Park, but it is a most worthwhile and easily accessible objective. The panoramic vista is extraordinary in extent, including peaks in the Polish Tatra Mountains. There's an enticing bonus in the shape of a typical mountain inn, Chata Kamenná, serving a wide assortment of refreshments. The ridge walk westwards is an absolute classic, moderately undulating, past granite tors and across grassland. The shorter walks make use of a chair lift to a point high on the mountainside above Jasná.

Start from the **Jasná car park** or **bus terminus** below the Hotel Grand. Walk up a path past the hotel to a road and turn right; follow it for a few hundred metres, then turn left along the access road to the **Hotel Liptov**. Bear left along the edge of the hotel's parking area for a few steps, to join a blue-waymarked path. It leads along the edge of the forest, above a derelict building, then becomes a trail through the forest. On coming to a wide **ski run**, follow a path to the right along the edge of the forest for approximately 20m, then bear left under a **ski tow** and cross the ski run on a clear path. Turn right and climb a path. At the upper end of a clump of conifers on your right, bear right across the slope, pass under the tow and follow a track into the forest (**26min**). The track gains height gradually; cross the edge of a ski run (**40min**) and continue on a forest path. This crosses two steams, the first via a bridge, the second on stepping stones, then ascends to a path junction, **Pod Orlou Skalou** (**1h2min**). From here follow the red-waymarked path steadily uphill, to a good **viewpoint** overlooking Jasná (**1h10min**). Continue up through dwarf pines, then past a **chair lift station** on the right. Go up steps and carry on a short distance to an intersection called **Luková** (**1h32min**). Follow the blue-waymarked path which zigzags uphill under a disused chair lift to **Chopok Úboč**, the terminus of the Záhradky chair lift (**1h52min**). *(Shorter walks 1 and 2 join here.)*

An excellent stone-paved path leads you onwards, soon quite close to the edge of the cliffs on the left, up past a deserted **chair lift station** and a large **communications installation**, over the crest and down slightly — to a liberally signposted path junction (**2h8min**). Here, among other routes, you join the **European long-distance walking route E8**, which runs from the Baltic to the Black Sea! From here it's only a few minutes along a good path to the bouldery summit of **Chopok** (**2h15min**; Picnic 16). An engraved metal plate helps with identification of features near and far, including peaks in the Slovakian High Tatras (Walks 11-19) and Malá Fatra National Park (Walks 26-31) to the northwest.

Descend to the popular **Kamenná Chata** (**2h22min**; varied menu in English, including fish and chips!). *(Shorter walk 1 turns back here.)*

Follow the well-made path waymarked in red generally westwards, initially across the southern slope, but soon on the grassy crest. It crosses a boulder field, skirting the rocky summit of **Dereše**, and leads to a slightly misleading sign, 'Dereše 2004m', from where it rises to almost that height on the western side of the summit (**2h47min**). The path then descends all the way down to **Sedlo Pol'any** (**3h30min**).

From the junction at this saddle head right on the yellow-marked path towards *Tri Vody*. The path descends, fairly steeply at first, into the narrow valley, then beside the tumbling stream, **Zadná Voda**. You cross a small log bridge and come to the **Tri Vody** path junction (**4h10min**). Descend some steps and cross two streams on stepping stones, beyond which an easier path leads into conifers. The path becomes a trail (**4h29min**) that carries you down, across two log bridges, and to a road opposite **Mikulášska Chata** (**4h50min**). Turn right and follow the road back downhill, past the access road to the **Hotel Liptov**, to the **bus stop and car park** near the Hotel Grand in **Jasná** (**5h**).

Walk 25 (Low Tatras): THE POL'ANA SPUR

See map on pages 108-109
Distance: 13.6km/8.4mi; 5h18min
Grade: moderate-strenuous (approximately 1000m/3300ft ascent); on signposted and waymarked minor roads, trails and paths
Equipment: see page 31
Refreshments: available in Jasná and probably at roadside bars and a hotel in the Demänová Valley at the end of the walk. Water bottles can be replenished at Tri Vody (use purifying tablets).
Transport: 🚗, or 🚆 and 🚌 to Jasná as for Walk 23 (page 108); return to Jasná by bus from Jaskyňa Slobody (see Transport, page 134).
Nearest accommodation: Demänová Valley, Jasná
Shorter walk: Pol'ana by chair lift. 12.9km/7.7mi; 4h58min. Moderate (approximately 470m/1542ft ascent). Equipment and refreshments as for the main walk (except for water at Tri Vody); transport as for Shorter walk 24-1 on page 111. Follow **Walk 24** from the 1h52min-point to **Sedlo Pol'any** (the 3h30min-point), then pick up the walk below at the 1h58min-point.

The chair lifts and ski tows on the mountainside directly above Jasná aren't ubiquitous, and it is possible to enjoy a day's walking far from the sight and sound of such fixtures, useful though they can be. The long high spur enclosing the Demänová Valley to the west provides such an opportunity, with an excellent traverse along its narrow spine. The descent finishes on a dramatic note, through a deep but easily passable gorge. The views in all directions are magnificent, extending to nearly all the High Tatras peaks on a good day.

Start in **Jasná**: follow Walk 23 (page 110) to **Tri Vody** (**58min**). Bear right at the junction here, to continue upstream on the yellow-waymarked route. The steep path climbs beside the stream, **Zadná Voda** — at first through conifer forest, but soon more in the open, as dwarf pines take over. The last part of the ascent to the main ridge is steep, but the path tackles the slope in a series of wide zigzags, up to the ridge and the gap called **Sedlo Pol'any** (**1h58min**). Continue up to the right with red waymarks, steeply at first, to the summit of **Pol'ana** (**2h10min**). Here you leave the ridge and turn northwards along a spur dotted with granite tors. Descend steeply then climb steadily, first on the eastern slope and then the crest. Soon you reach the top of **Zák-l'uky** (**2h30min**) from where, among much else, Vrbické Pleso, the small lake in Jasná, is visible far below. The path leads on across a small tor, down and up again on the eastern flank above a deep, pine-filled basin, and on to the flat summit of **Bôr** (**2h54min**). The High Tatras seem much closer from here, beyond the lake,

View east to Chopok from above Sedlo Pol'any (Walks 24 and 25)

Liptovská Mara, in the valley below to the north. The descent now begins in earnest, at first through dense clumps of dwarf pine interspersed with small grassy glades, then through tall conifer forest. Beyond a minor saddle (**3h 30min**), the path follows a tortuous (but well-waymarked) route down through the forest, rich in autumn-sprouting fungi.

Eventually you reach **Sedlo Pod Sinou** (**4h18min**), where you turn right (still with yellow waymarks). The path traverses downhill across the mountainside, first to the left then back to the right. Then *take care* to follow a change in direction, as the route plummets directly down to a small stream. Cross this just above its junction with a larger stream (**4h48min**). Continue down beside the larger stream briefly; then enjoy a short stretch along a good trail before descending a steep, rough path. You cross the stream four times, passing tall limestone cliffs, and follow the path into a small **gorge**. Continue down, with the stream below on the right, then cross it twice more. Beyond a small **river gauging station** you suddenly meet a minor road. Bear left for a few steps to the main valley road; the **bus stop** is nearby to the left, opposite **Jaskyňa Slobody** and the Hotel FIM (**5h18min**).

View south along the spur, from near the summit of Bôr

MALÁ FATRA NATIONAL PARK

Malá Fatra (Walks 26-31) is the westernmost national park featured in this guide and is separated from the Tatra Mountains by the broad Orava Valley. Though essentially mountainous in character, the summits are generally much lower than in the other mountain parks. The 22,600ha/55,800 acre park was set aside in 1988, principally to protect the flora and fauna dependent on its varied geology. Rounded contours and shallow saddles indicate crystalline rocks (schist, gneiss), while hard limestones are visible in rugged cliffs and narrow ridges. Where underground limestone caverns *(diery)* have been cut by streams, gorges have developed, notably the gorges of Nové, Dolné and Horné Diery (see Walk 30).

The core of the park is a long east/west ridge from which rises the highest peak in the park, Vel'ký Kriváň (1709m). The extensive forests on the lower and middle slopes comprise mainly beech; at higher levels, far-reaching grasslands are interspersed with small areas of dwarf pine. There are way-marked paths and trails along the central ridge, several of the long spurs extending south from the ridge, and through some of the valleys below.

The large town of Žilina is the transport hub nearest to the area. Trains from (and to) Bratislava (and some from Prague in the Czech Republic), stop here at least every two hours. From the east, trains from Spišská Nová Ves (Slovenský Raj), Poprad (Slovakia's High Tatras) and Liptovský Mikuláš (Low Tatras) also stop here at least every two hours. Long-distance buses ply the route between Poprad, Liptovský Mikuláš, Žilina, and Bratislava with several daily departures.

The SAD bus service operates numerous services Mon-Fri (fewer on weekends) between Žilina and Terchová, a very small town immediately to the north of the park in the Varínka Valley. This, and perhaps the small village of Štefanová within the park itself, are the natural bases for exploring the Malá Fatra. See transport details for Walks 26-31 on page 134; locally, consult the tourist office in Terchová, where time-tables are on display, and English-speaking staff can provide guidance.

Walk 26 (Malá Fatra): THE ASCENT OF KRAVIARSKE

Distance: 8.3km/5.1mi; 4h10min
Grade: moderate-strenuous (924m/3030ft ascent); on signposted road, trails and paths; the paths can become very slippery after rain. One short section, with chain and metal handrails, crosses a short log bridge, but it is *not* exposed or difficult.
Equipment: see page 31
Refreshments: available at Chata Vrátna and at Starý Dvor
Transport: 🚗 (Car tours 6 and 7) or 🚌 (see page 115 and Transport, page 134) to Terchová and then on to Chata Vrátna. By car, leave Terchová approximately 150m east of the prominent church and drive south along the road signposted to 'Ski Centrum Vrátna'. The road runs through the Tiesňavy Gorge and up the valley to a parking area on the right (5.2km) at a place called Stará Dolina; a fee may be charged.
🚌: the bus stop in Terchová is outside the post office, about 50m east of the prominent church. Return by 🚌 from Starý Dvor — to Terchová or up to the car park at Stará Dolina.
Nearest accommodation: Terchová, Štefanová

Not without its ups and downs, this walk offers a very scenic introduction to the Malá Fatra National Park. It takes you up to and along the spur enclosing the valley Vrátna Dolina, from where there are good views of the long east-west ridge in the heart of the park and of the elongated spurs reaching north into the Varínka Valley. Each spur is punctuated by distinct saddles and prominent, usually rocky peaks, notably rugged Vel'ký Rozsutec to the east.

Start the walk from the **bus terminus** below **Chata Vrátna**: walk back downhill for 0.5km, past the **Stará Dolina car park**, to the nearby start of a green-waymarked route signposted to *Sedlo za Kraviarskym*. Cross a wide **log bridge** and, almost immediately, bear right up a broad trail in conifer forest, past a line of low cliffs. Climbing steadily, the trail bends left to cross a small gully, then right, and continues gaining height southwestwards (**17min**). From around here, conifers give way to beech and sycamore, a transition that's particularly striking in autumn.

Willow-leaved gentian

The trail becomes a path and, beyond a small **log bridge**, the gradient steepens (**28min**); soon you're climbing beside the stream bed on the left (**35min**). After a short while the path swings northwards to zigzag steeply up the side of the adjacent spur (**43min**), gaining the crest on the edge of open ground (**53min**). There's scant respite, and soon you're climbing through low conifers to reach the crest of the spur at **Sedlo za Kraviarskym** (**1h20min**). There are even benches at this saddle, from which to enjoy the fine view dominated by the crags and cliffs of Veľký Rozsutec to the east.

Turn right with blue waymarks, to climb northwards along a pleasantly unworn path to the summit of **Kraviarske** (**1h45min**), another fine vantage point, from where the village of Štefanová below Veľký Rozsutec is also in view.

Soon the spur narrows and the steep, rather rocky descent begins, down to an open saddle (**Veľké**

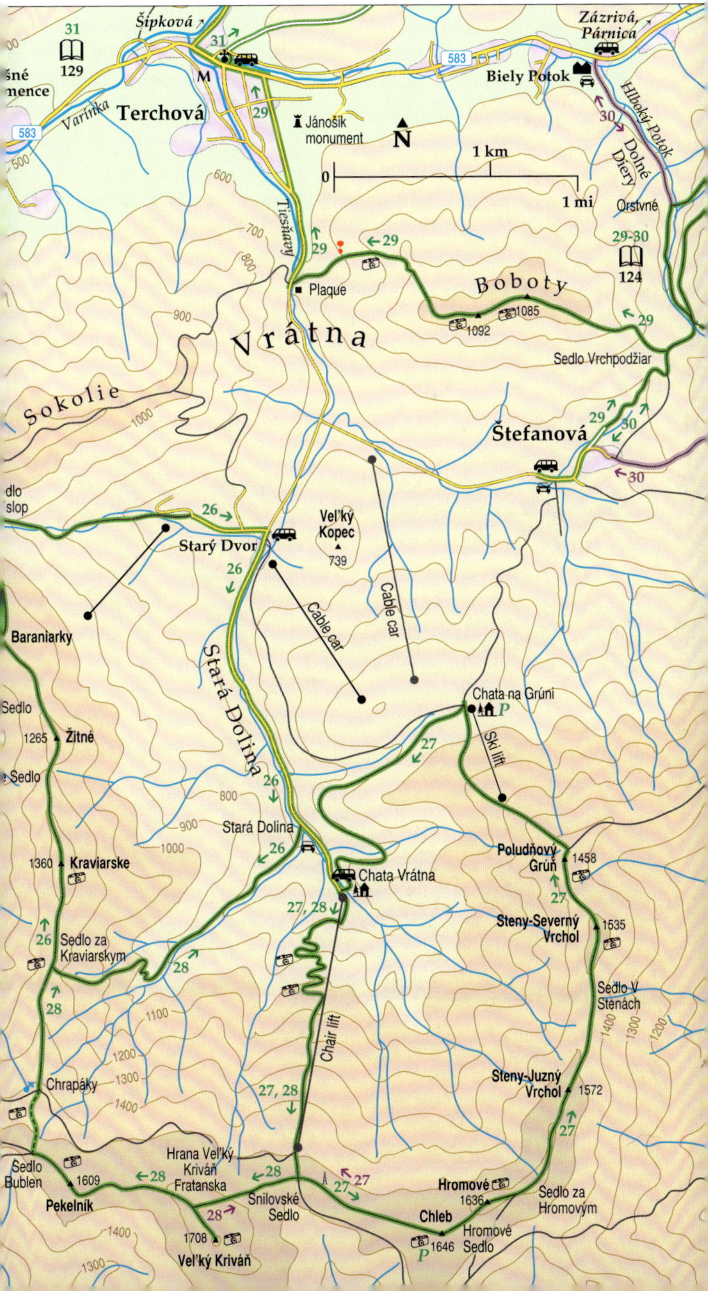

Sedlo; **2h10min**). In autumn, all the way along the spur (and elsewhere in Malá Fatra), ripe bilberries lie in wait to tempt you! Continue straight up to the wooded summit of **Žitné** (**2h20min**). From here the path drops to **Malé Sedlo** (**2h38min**) and, almost inevitably, climbs straight up to the base of a small bluff. Traversing to the left, you come to **handrails and a log bridge** no more than 5m long. A few metres beyond it, climb a slope and rock steps up to the small pinnacle that is **Baraniarky**, another first-class lookout, from where the Sokolie ridge dominates the view ahead (**3h2min**).

From the pinnacle it's a long steep descent through beech forest to **Sedlo Prislop** (**3h32min**), with a view of Veľký Rozsutec and Štefanová. The last downhill stretch is comparatively easy and mostly in the open. Join a track (**3h50min**) and go on past the base of a ski lift to a minor road (**4h**). Continue down to the main road at **Starý Dvor** (**4h10min**); the **Stará Dolina car park** is 1.7km up to the right.

Walk 27 (Malá Fatra): THE ASCENT OF CHLEB

See photographs opposite and on page 39 and 122
Distance: 11km/6.8mi; 4h47min
Grade: strenuous (1129m/3700ft ascent); on signposted and waymarked trails and paths, some of which (particularly on the descent from Chata na Grúni) may be slippery when wet.
Equipment: see page 31
Refreshments: available at Chata Vrátna and Chata na Grúni.
Transport: (Car tours 6 and 7) or (see page 115 and Transport, page 134) to Terchová and then on to Chata Vrátna. By car, leave Terchová approximately 150m east of the prominent church and drive south along the road signposted to 'Ski Centrum Vrátna'. The road runs through the Tiesňavy Gorge and up the valley to a parking area on the right (5.2km) at a place called Stará Dolina; a fee may be charged. : the bus stop in Terchová is outside the post office, about 50m east of the prominent church. Use the same transport to return.
Nearest accommodation: Terchová, Štefanová
Shorter walks: The chair lift to near Snilovské Sedlo, being upgraded at time of writing, will be open in 2006, making these shorter walks possible.
1 Chleb by chair lift. 2.4km/1.5mi; 58min. Easy (146m/480ft ascent). Equipment: see page 31; refreshments available at Chata Vrátna; transport as for the main walk as far as Chata Vrátna, then chair lift. From the top lift station, join the main walk at the 1h41min-point, walk on to Chleb, and return the same way.
2 Main walk from Snilovské Sedlo. 7.9km/4.9mi; 3h10min. Moderate (305m/1000ft ascent). Equipment, refreshments as main walk; transport as for Shorter walk 1. From the top lift station, join the main walk at the 1h41min-point and follow it to the end.

Chleb (1646m) is the third highest peak in Malá Fatra National Park. If its name derives from the word for bread *(chlieb),* the reason is a mystery — can you see any resemblance to a loaf of bread? Irrespective of such speculations, it's a worthy objective for a day's outing, affording very wide-ranging views. The walk along part of the high, moderately undulating ridge is superb, with the wonderful experience of enjoying a bird's-eye view of the valleys far below to both north and south. Chata na Grúni, about two-thirds of the way back down, is ideally placed for restorative refreshments.

Start the walk from **Chata Vrátna** by going up the minor road past the *chata* entrance, following a green-waymarked route. Turn right in front of the first two-storey house on the left. Cross a **bridge** and follow a path uphill. It passes beneath the chair lift (**8min**) and becomes more of a trail, with well-designed zigzags up through the forest. At the end of the trail, almost beneath the **chair lift** (**38min**), bear slightly right up a path which goes under the cables to climb more steeply, then back under the lift and up to the edge of a clearing (**48min**). Soon you enjoy excellent views of Tiesňavy Gorge in the Vrátna Valley and Terchová beyond (**1h**).

Left: Veľký Rozsutec and the main ridge towards Poludňový Grúň (Walk 27)

Eventually the path leaves scattered dwarf pines behind (**1h28min**) and soon reaches the **top station of the chair lift** (**1h41min**). *(Both Shorter walks join here.)*

Skirt the station on the uphill side, to reach a cobbled path which leads easily up a grassy saddle (**Snilovské Sedlo;1h46min**) and a signposted intersection. Continue to the left (east) along the red-waymarked route, past a small **communications tower** and through clumps of dwarf pine. The ridge narrows as the route negotiates a rock outcrop, then climbs easily to the summit of **Chleb** (**2h12min**; Picnic 17). The views to the east of the wide Orava Valley give an entirely new perspective to the location of the Malá Fatra range.

Inevitably you have to descend, past a rocky knob, across the small gap called **Hromové Sedlo**, and then up to the grassy top of **Hromové** (**2h25min**), only 10m lower than Chleb. The path then descends to the next small gap, from where you can either climb over **Steny-Juzný Vrchol** or bypass it (to the right). There follows a steep descent to the next gap (**Sedlo V Stenách**; **3h5min**), followed by a steady climb to **Steny-Severný Vrchol** (**3h 20min**), from which the prospect of Vel'ký Rozsutec is particularly impressive.

The ensuing descent to a signposted junction at **Poludňový Grún** (**3h31min**) is straightforward. Continue steeply downhill, following a yellow-waymarked route, mostly across open ground. The path (or network of parallel paths) tends to the right, descending through scattered trees — to the homely **Chata na Grúni** (**4h12min**; Picnic 18). On the Slovak-German menu, the words 'Big Cappuccino' leapt out, and I can assure you it is big, delicious and remarkably inexpensive!

For the final stretch, continue from a signposted intersection just beyond the *chata;* turn left (southwestwards), to follow the yellow-waymarked route, initially marked by low yellow poles, down the left-hand side of a small valley. Clearly defined all the way, it crosses a spur, traverses another smaller valley, then descends to **Chata Vrátna** (**4h47min**).

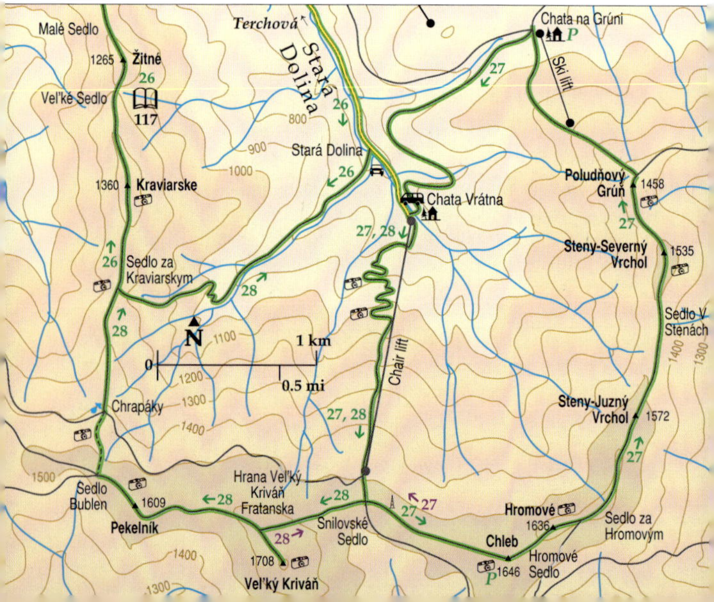

Walk 28 (*Malá Fatra*): THE ASCENT OF VEL'KÝ KRIVÁŇ

See map opposite
Distance: 9.7km/6mi; 4h30min
Grade: strenuous (989m/3245ft ascent); on signposted and waymarked paths, trails and tracks
Equipment: see page 31
Refreshments: available at Chata Vrátna; water bottles may be replenished close to Chrapáky (the 3h20min-point).
Transport: 🚘 or 🚌 as Walk 27, page 119
Nearest accommodation: Terchová, Štefanová
Shorter walks: At time of writing the chair lift to near Snilovské Sedlo was being upgraded, and I was assured by the helpful tourist office staff in Terchová that it would be open in 2006, making these shorter walks possible.

1 Vel'ký Kriváň by chair lift. 2.6km/1.6mi; 1h26min. Easy (209m/685ft ascent). Equipment: see page 31; refreshments available at Chata Vrátna; transport as for the main walk as far as Chata Vrátna, then chair lift. From the top lift station, join the main walk at the 1h41min-point and follow it to 2h41min-point, then retrace steps to the chair lift to return to Chata Vrátna.

2 Main walk from Snilovské Sedlo. 6.8km/4.2mi; 2h49min. Moderate (239m/785ft ascent). Equipment, refreshments as main walk. Transport as for Shorter walk 1. From the top lift station, join the main walk at the 1h41min-point and follow it to the end.

Vel'ký Kriváň (1709m) is the highest peak in the Malá Fatra National Park, the apex of the long central ridge. The ascent is very popular and well worth the effort for the extensive panoramic view. The purists' approach, on foot all the way from Chata Vrátna, is described as the main walk. But the chair lift to just below Snilovské Sedlo provides an easier alternative, saving approximately 750m/2460ft ascent.

Start by following **Walk 27** (page 119) to the top of the **chair lift** (**1h41min**). *(Shorter Walks 1 and 2 join here.)* Take the stone-paved path up to a signposted intersection at **Snilovské Sedlo** (**1h 46min**). Continue up to the right (west) along a broad, red-waymarked trail; it climbs steadily to a signposted junction on the left called **Hrana Vel'ký Kriváň Fratanska** (**2h4min**). From here a wide path leads left up the gravelly slope to the lumpy summit ridge, and on to the somewhat amorphous summit of **Vel'ký Kriváň** (**2h24min**). With luck you'll be able to see all the main features in the Malá Fatra National Park and even the High Tatra Mountains across the broad Orava Valley.

Return to the path junction (**2h41min**). *(Shorter Walk 1 returns to the chair lift from here.)* Turn left, still with red waymarks, to descend the rather slender ridge. The path leads on across the southern side of the crest, then switches to the opposite slope. It then rises across two distinct 'knobs' and traverses the narrow crest, with a steep drop to the south, to reach the summit of **Pekelník**.

The ridge now veers markedly to the right (northwest), affording a fine view west to Malý Kriváň. Descend to **Sedlo Bublen** (**3h6min**) and from this saddle take the well-used (but unsignposted and unwaymarked) path heading northwards — down the side of a spur initially, then on the broad crest, with a magnificent view of the Tiesňavy Gorge. You descend steeply to a signposted junction called **Chrapáky** (**3h20min**), where a sign, 'Voda', pointing to the left, alerts you to a water source.

Continue steeply down with blue waymarks to **Sedlo za Kraviarskym** (**3h34min**). From here, where the waymark colour is green, turn right (east) down through dwarf pines and into beech forest (**3h50min**). The path leads down the very steep slope easily enough, to a **stream** (**3h58min**). Continue down, with the stream on your right. Soon you're on a rocky trail which leads to a **log bridge** (**4h10min**) and on to a track into a wider valley, another **log bridge**, and the road (**4h30min**). The **Stará Dolina car park** is 60m to the right, and the bus stop at **Chata Vrátna** is just a five-minute walk away.

The Tiesňavy Gorge from the ascent to Snilovské Sedlo (Walks 27 and 28)

Walk 29 (*Malá Fatra*): THE TRAVERSE OF BOBOTY RIDGE

Distance: 5.9km/3.7mi; 2h50min
Grade: moderate (approximately 500m/1640ft ascent); on signposted and waymarked paths and trails, and a road. There are fixed chain handrails on two sections during the final part of the descent from Boboty: the first can be bypassed; the protection afforded on the second stretch could be useful for reassurance, but neither place is exposed.
Equipment: see page 31
Refreshments: available at Štefanová, Koliba Podžiar (a three-minute walk downhill from Sedlo Vrchpodžiar) and Terchová

Transport: See Walk 27 on page 119 for access to Terchová. 🚗 Travelling by car, follow the road from Terchová towards Chata Vrátna (as for Walk 27), but turn left (2.5km) at a signposted junction, to reach a large parking area on the edge of the village of Štefanová (4.1km). 🚌 from Terchová to Štefanová (see Transport, page 134); the bus stop in Terchová is outside the post office, about 50m east of the prominent church.
Nearest accommodation: Štefanová, Terchová

Boboty is a rugged isolated massif between Terchová and the village of Štefanová, its pinnacles and cliffs forming the eastern ramparts of the Tiesňavy Gorge at the entrance to the Vrátna Valley. Its eastern slopes rise almost as impressively from Dolné Diery (see Walk 30 overleaf). The traverse of its crest provides a scenic and interesting walk, as the path winds around tall limestone pinnacles and large boulders which play host to a rich variety of mosses, lichens, flowering plants and even small trees. Don't be deterred by the reference to chains above: there are many good hand- and foot-holds on the dissected cliffs to which they're fixed.

Start the walk from the **car park** or adjacent **bus stop** at **Štefanová**: follow the road into the village. After about 100m go straight ahead at a junction for another 200m, then bear left with yellow waymarks along an unsurfaced road which soon becomes a path. Cross a **bridge** (**10min**), climb to a junction, and bear left along a track to another junction at a saddle (**Sedlo Vrchpodžiar**; **22min**). (Note that refreshments are available at Koliba Podžiar, a log cabin three minutes' walk downhill to the right from here.)

Follow the green-waymarked path up the grassy slope (westwards), past **old wooden buildings** and into conifer forest. The path winds up the steep slope, with conifers gradually yielding prominence to beeches. The gradient slackens slightly once the path gains a distinct crest (**42min**); it takes you up to the summit ridge and a good lookout on the left above Štefanová (**1h7min**). The path easily negotiates a dissected rock outcrop, passes an isolated tor, and climbs to the signposted but view-less high point of '**Boboty 1085m**'.

Continue down on the path — a deep carpet of pine needles — then regain some height, coming to two almost adjacent **vantage points** (**1h21min**). The path then descends to the right and stays below the tors and pinnacles on the crest until it reaches another **lookout** (**1h32min**). The descent continues, again below the crest,

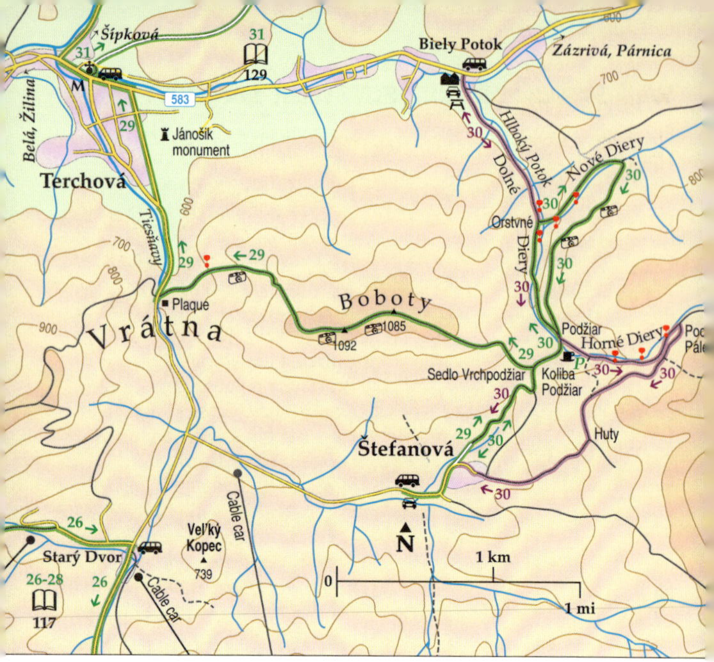

on the northern side; look out for a good view of the early stages of Walk 31 from a gap in the trees (**1h47min**).

Continue down, steeply now, past a large pinnacle; soon the Tiesňavy cliffs and the road come into view (**2h3min**). The path leads along the foot of a low cliff to the first set of **chain handrails**; the top one is superfluous and easily bypassed; either circumvent the lower one via the grassy slope on the right, or go down backwards, holding the chain in both hands.

The narrow path then descends on the slender crest to a rather eroded gully and slope, overlooked by an enormous pinnacle, and with **another set of chains**, very much an optional extra (**2h16min**). From here the path winds easily down into the forested valley and leads on to the **Vrátna Valley road** (**2h36min**). Walk left up the road for about 100m, to where a plaque on the cliff marks the height of floodwaters which destroyed part of Štefanová in 1848. Return to **Terchová** along the road (**2h50min**).

The Tiesňavy Gorge from Boboty ridge

Walk 30 (Malá Fatra): DOLNÉ DIERY AND NOVÉ DIERY

See map opposite
Distance: 6.4km/4mi; 2h20min
Grade: moderate (240m/785ft ascent); on signposted and waymarked paths, a road and an unsurfaced road. *You must have a head for heights:* you will climb metal ladders (with handrails) and cross narrow metal bridges over streams and above waterfalls. Shorter walk 2 (with only one ladder) is a possible alternative.
Equipment: see page 31
Refreshments: available at Štefanová and Koliba Podžiar
Transport: as Walk 27, page 119 to Terchová. By car, follow the road towards Chata Vrátna, but turn left (2.5km) at a signposted junction, to reach a large parking area on the edge of the village of Štefanová (4.1km). (see Transport, page 134) from Terchová to Štefanová; the Terchová bus stop in is outside the post office, about 50m east of the prominent church .
Nearest accommodation: Terchová, Štefanová
Shorter walks
1 Dolné Diery and Nové Diery from Biely Potok. 5km/3mi; 1h 50min. Easy (130m/425ft ascent). Equipment: see page 31; refreshments at Biely Potok and Koliba Podžiar. Transport: (see Transport, page 134) or to Biely Potok, 2.7km east along the main road from Terchová; park in front of the Hotel Diery (a fee may be charged). From the main road in **Biely Potok**, set out along a signposted, blue-waymarked trail, past the hotel on your right, then a **picnic area**. Cross a bridge and follow the trail upstream to a second bridge (**8min**) and then a third bridge, where the valley closes in. Follow the path beside the stream, **Hlboký Potok**, to two more bridges, the second at the entrance to **Dolné Diery** (**19min**). Cross the stream again, then follow a path along the base of the high gorge wall; the path gives way to a **bridge-cum-walkway** through the gorge (barely 3m wide at this point), and on to a path junction called **Ostrvné** (**21min**). Join the main walk here and follow it from the 1h1min-point to the 1h55min-point near **Koliba Podžiar** (refreshments). To return to Biely Potok, follow the main walk from the 29min-point back down to **Ostrvné**, then retrace steps to Biely Potok.
2 Biely Potok to Štefanová. 3.6km/2.2mi; 1h10min. Easy (185m/600ft ascent). Equipment: see page 31; refreshments at Biely Potok, Koliba Podžiar and Štefanová. Transport: from Terchová to Biely Potok, and from Štefanová back to Terchová (see Transport on page 134). Follow **Shorter walk 1 to Ostrvné** (**21min**). Continue to the right, upstream, along a path at the base of the cliff, to a ladder. From the top of the ladder a **metal bridge-cum-walkway** traverses beside the cliff to a proper bridge. Con-

Ladder in Horné Diery (Alternative and Longer walks)

tinue along the edge of the stream, up to another bridge, then a cluster of boulders, then another bridge. A streamside path leads you **out of the gorge (35min)**; from here it's easy going up to a path junction called **Podžiar**. Cross the stream to a log cabin, **Koliba Podžiar (47min)**, then follow the yellow-waymarked path uphill to **Sedlo Vrchpodžiar (51min)**. Shortly after this saddle, turn right at a junction and follow the woodland path down to and through the village of **Štefanová** to the **bus stop (1h10min)**.

Alternative walk: Horné Diery. 4.8km/2.9mi; 1h59min. Moderate (215m/705ft ascent). Equipment, refreshments and transport as for the main walk.Follow the **main walk to Podžiar (29min)**. From this junction, make your way into **Horné Diery**: follow a narrow path up through a field; cross two bridges and continue up into beech forest. Beyond another bridge, negotiate steps cut into the rock, climb two ladders and cross **bridges above waterfalls** to a third ladder; continue up beside the cascade to a small sloping crag with a chain to help you up, then traverse the stream bed. Negoiate a cluster of boulders with comparative ease, cross two bridges and climb a long **ladder above a waterfall**. There follows a series of **steps cut into the rock**, only some of which have an accompanying handrail — the most awkward section of all. Continue around a bend to the left (**30min**) and soon you're in **another gorge**. Cross the stream and climb two fairly long flights of steps, then two more inconsequential series of steps.Soon you reach a path junction called **Pod Pálenicou (43min)** and the end of the fun. Bear right along a yellow-waymarked route towards *Štefanová,* to follow a pleasantly easy path in forest, initially above Horné Diery; further on you can glimpse Koliba Podžiar far below (**59min**). At a path junction called **Huty (1h8min)**, bear right downhill with green waymarks; the route is sparsely waymarked, but the route followed by other walkers is clear on the ground, more or less straight down for a few minutes, then heading left for a short distance. Continue directly down, and you soon emerge into the open with Štefanová in view (**1h12min**). Go on through a narrow belt of trees, then down along the edge of a field, Meet a track and follow it through **Štefanová** to a junction; turn left along a road to the **bus stop/car park (1h30min)**.

Longer walk: Include Horné Diery in the main walk (7.9km/5mi; 3h23min; moderate, with (395m/1295ft ascent). At the 1h53min-point in the main walk, continue straight ahead, following the Alternative walk from the 29min-point to the end.

Here is an unusual opportunity to walk through two gorges, rather than to look down on them from the heights of a ridge or mountaintop. Perhaps 'walk' is not the best word to describe the descent of Dolné Diery (Lower Caverns) and ascent of Nové Diery (New Caverns) by means of securely-fixed metal bridges-cum-walkways and ladders with handrails. Not being particularly comfortable in airy places, I set foot on the first ladder rather tentatively but very soon was exhilarated by the experience of scaling waterfalls and crossing tumbling streams. If you really enjoy this, then

Horné Diery (Upper Caverns; Alternative or Longer walks) is recommended. It's even more exciting and perhaps more scenic, as the gorge is surrounded by beech rather than conifers. On the other hand, Shorter walk 2 offers an introduction to Malá Fatra gorge-walking, but with only one ladder to scale. Ten interpretive panels in Slovak and English earnestly describe various natural features and some local history en route. Both Shorter walks start from the hamlet of Biely Potok, a few kilometres east of Terchová along the main road.

Starting at the **Štefanová bus stop/car park**, walk along the road into the village; 100m along you come to a signposted junction where there's a large information board introducing the **Diery Interpretive Trail**. Continue almost straight ahead along the road for approximately 200m to another junction. Bear left here, following yellow waymarks along an unsurfaced road which soon becomes a path, with Malý and Vel'ký Rozsutec towering impressively almost overhead.

Cross a **bridge** (**10min**), climb to a junction and turn left along a track (**21min**) to another junction at a saddle (**Sedlo Vrchpodžiar**; **22min**). Continue ahead, then down to **Koliba Podžiar** (**27min**; Picnic 19), a log cabin half hidden in tall trees. Go down to the nearby stream, cross a **log bridge**, and reach a junction called **Podžiar** (**29min**). Turn left here, along the lower, blue-waymarked path. *(But for the Alternative walk, turn right.)*

The blue path leads into **Dolné Diery**, descends past two information boards, crosses a couple of bridges and skirts some low cliffs on the left. Cross another **bridge** (**42min**), negotiate a rocky stretch, then descend beside a waterfall to a bridge. Make your way down a rock outcrop to the next bridge, which leads you into a small **gorge**. Cross a bridge almost directly above a cascade, and another beside the cliff, then follow steps cut into the rock (with handrail) to the first metal ladder, which looks more daunting than it actually is. This takes you down to a junction called **Ostrvné** (**1h1min**). *(Shorter walk 1 joins here.)*

Turn right upstream into **Nové Diery**. Soon you're traversing a gorge with the help of steps and bridges with handrails. Then, around a sharp bend, the gorge narrows to barely 2m wide; steps and bridges lead to a long ladder — exciting or challenging, depending on your disposition! This takes you up to a ramp, then some solid rock, a short ladder and a bridge through another tight squeeze — and suddenly the excitement's over (**1h18min**)!

Cross a bridge and bear right (beside an information board about rare and endangered species) and continue generally uphill to a railed **lookout** directly above the gorge (**1h27min**). Continue up, soon heading right across the steep slope. Beyond a panel about birds, you come to another **lookout** (**1h43min**) over the fields near Štefanová. Continue downhill, back to the **Podžiar** junction (**1h53min**). *(The Alternative walk continues to the right here; the Longer walk carries on straight ahead.)*

Cross to **Koliba Podžiar** (**1h55min**), then retrace your steps via **Sedlo Vrchpodžiar**. Turn right at the next junction, down to **Štefanová** (**2h20min**).

Walk 31 (Malá Fatra): THE JURAJ JÁNOŠÍK WALK

Distance: 14.9km/9.2mi; 4h15min
Grade: moderate (430m/1410ft ascent) on waymarked roads, unsurfaced roads, tracks, trails and paths
Equipment: see page 31
Refreshments: available in Terchová and Šípková
Transport: 🚗 (Car tours 6 and 7) or 🚌 (see page 115) to/from Terchová. There is no designated parking area in the village; the best bet is to leave Terchová approximately 150m east of the prominent church and drive south along the road signposted to 'Ski Centrum Vrátna', then park about 150m along, in the area adjacent to the Coop supermarket
Nearest accommodation: Terchová

Shorter walks
1 Terchová to Šípková. 6.5km/4mi; 2h28min. Easy-moderate (290m/950ft ascent). Equipment, refreshments and transport as for the main walk, then return by 🚌 from Šípková to Terchová (see Transport, page 134). Follow the main walk to the 2h28min-point at **Šípková** and return to Terchová by bus.
2 Šípková to Terchová. 8.4km/5.2mi; 1h47min. Easy-moderate (140m/450ft ascent). Equipment and refreshments as for the main walk. Transport: 🚌 from Terchová to Šípková (see Transport, page, 134). Join the main walk at the **Šípková** (the 2h28min-point); walk back to Terchová.

Juraj Jánošík could be described as Slovakia's national hero, an 18th-century rebel in the Robin Hood mould, who was horribly executed in Liptovský Mikuláš in 1713. He hailed from a small village in the hills a few miles north of Terchová and is celebrated locally with a huge aluminium statue above the Vrátna Valley road, and a small museum. He was also the inspiration for the creation of a walking route through his countryside, passing by several villages including his own. Nine information boards along the way describe folklore, wooden houses, the man himself, various aspects of farming, and local natural and cultural features. Another board, between Terchová's church and the main bus stop, introduces the walk; summary English translations are provided.

As a substantial bonus, the views across the Varínka Valley to the Malá Fatra mountains, especially Veľký and Malý Rozsutec, are superb. The walk divides neatly into two sections at the village of Šípková at the end of a bus route. The route is waymarked with white squares or arrows crossed by a green diagonal line; it is alone among the walks based at Terchová in being outside Malá Fatra National Park.

You start in **Terchová**, on the eastern side of the large **church** on the main road, along a path between the church wall and a stream, **Biely Potok**. The narrow path leads around a corner of the wall, skirting the church grounds, to flights of steps. At the top, turn right along a rough track; shortly, bear right at a junction and climb steeply. The track veers right then left, less steeply, up to **notice board No 2** (**15min**; Picnic 20), from where you continue up a clear path along a wide strip of grass.

Just short of the crest of the spur known as **Úboč**, bear right

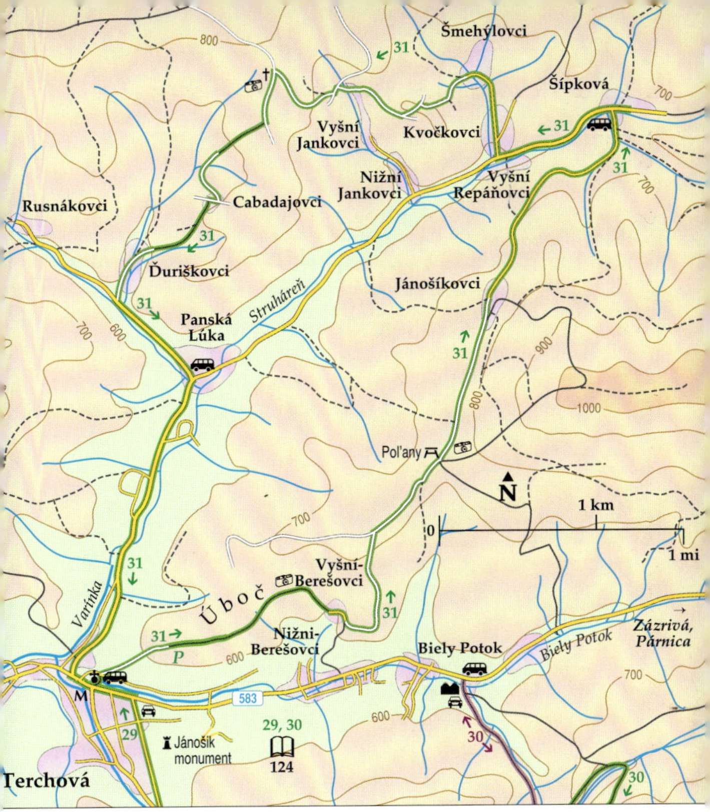

through scattered bushes, soon reaching more or less flat ground. The path swings left (**30min**) and descends to a junction. Turn right and follow a trail across fields and down to the hamlet of **Vyšní-Berešovci** (**57min**). About 50m past the last house, bear left along a track which soon bends left and climbs a steep spur to a slight saddle, a junction and **notice board No 3** (**1h22min**). Continue to the right along a track, past a collection of farm buildings (the fiercely barking dogs are chained), rising slightly to a junction. Turn right along an unsurfaced road to a signposted junction called **Poľany** (**1h44min**), complete with a picnic table, near a large old farm house. Continue along the unsurfaced road, signposted to *Šípková,* soon passing through the dispersed village of **Jánošíkovci** (**1h47min**).

The part-surfaced road descends with good views of the valley below. At a junction beside some houses (**2h15min**), turn left and continue down to a road on the edge of **Šípková** village. At a signposted junction turn left to reach the **bus stop** (**2h28min**). *(Shorter walk 1 returns from here; Shorter walk 2 joins here.)* Follow the road downhill; the last house on the left, **Chata Šípková**, may be open for refreshments. At the hamlet of **Vyšní Repáňovci** (**2h36min**), turn right; then, beyond a rustic bar, turn left along a road; this leads into the village of **Šmehýlovci**, near a small sawmill. The road bends left uphill (**2h44min**) between houses, mainly old buildings in a traditional style, to a minor junction (**2h52min**) where, appropriately, there's an **information board** about Carpathian wooden houses.

House in Vyšní-Berešovci and (below) Statue of Juraj Jánošík above Terchová

Bear left along a track which then bends left and ascends, soon steeply, through fields. At a **waymark post (2h55min)**, turn right along a track and gain height across a sloping field. Reaching another track on the crest of a spur (**3h3min**), turn left. Descend steeply to a junction (**3h8min**); turn right and promptly climb steeply between wooden buildings in the village of **Vyšní-Jankovci**. A few metres past **information board No 8** on the right, cross a small stream and follow a track up to an intersection. Turn left and go up to and across the top of a field. At an indistinct junction, bear left, with a good view of Veľký and Malý Rozsutec. The track leads through a belt of trees, across a small field and through more trees to a larger field; continue in the open, straight up a grassy slope.

Almost at the top, bear left up to a track beside a small **oratory** (**3h18min**) and a group of buildings on the crest, where you turn left. Continue uphill; from the top corner of a vegetable garden on the right, strike up across the fields to the right (southwestwards). A grassy trail soon materialises beside a low bank on the left: follow this to a track (**3h22min**).

Walk down the track to an unsurfaced road beside farm buildings at the settlement of **Cabadajovci** (**3h27min**). Turn right, then left (**notice board No 9** is a few steps to the right) and go directly downhill on a path. This soon leads to the right (just past an incongruous street light). At an indistinct junction, with a hedge on the right, bear left and continue, soon into forest. Then descend a path beside a small stream to the village of **Durīškovci**. Follow a track which becomes an unsurfaced road, bending left down through the village. When you meet a road (**3h43min**), turn left. This leads down to a junction at the hamlet of **Panská Lúka** (**3h51min**) where there's a **bus stop**.

Turn right; the road (mostly with a parallel footpath) provides an interesting walk back to Terchová, past a variety of houses, mostly modern and seemingly quite prosperous. You reach the main road in **Terchová** 250m west of the **church** (**4h15min**).

BUSES

Poland

Bus services are operated by the national company Polska Komunikacja Samochodowa (PKS). Details of services operating from Zakopane are available at www.pks.zakopane.pl and from Nowy Targ at www.ppks.nowytarg.pl (both sites in Polish only). Click on 'Rozkład jazdy' for timetable information; see the key to the accompanying code letters below. The most important Polish word to remember is *Odjazdu* (departures).

Otherwise, timetables are displayed at the central bus stations in Zakopane and Nowy Targ; relevant timetables are also posted at each bus stop. The excellent tourist information office in Zakopane (tel +48 18 201 2211; Ulica Kościuszki 17), where most of the staff speak some English, can also help with timetable information — more so than anyone at the bus station.

The following slightly abridged key should help to demystify bus timetables; remember than *Roman numerals are used for months.*

The summary information about departures given on pages 132-134 *ignores* services that do not operate in Dec-Jan and at Easter.

Key to timetable coding

A	No services on Sun/holidays
D	No services Christmas, Easter
F	Operates Mon-Fri except public holidays
H	Operates during school and other holidays
K, N	No services at Christmas, Easter
L, U	No services at Christmas, New Year, Easter
Nh	No services Christmas or Easter Saturday
S	Operates during school term
Q	No service 23 Dec, 24 Dec, Easter Saturday
+	Operates Sun/holidays
*	Operates as announced
a	Operates from 1/7-31/8
b	Operates from 1/6-30/9
c	Operates from 28/5-30/9
d	Operates from 1/6-30/9 and from 20/12-30/4.
e	Operates from 15/6-20/9
k	Operates Mon-Fri except public holidays from 1/10-31/12
l	Operates from 27/12-28/2 and from 20/6-31/8
m	No service Christmas Eve and New Year's Eve
n	As m, plus Easter Saturday
r	No service at Corpus Christi (a Thursday in May or June)
5, 7	Operates Fri, Sun

Entries in red: express services

Other symbols relate to services between the places cited

Slovakia

Most bus services are operated by the national company Slovenská Autobusová Doprava (SAD); Eurolines operates services on some long distance routes. Timetables are displayed at bus stations and intermediate bus stops. Little if any timetable information is available on-line; it's most unlikely that you'll find anyone at the stations who can speak English. In this quandary, the local tourist office is the best source of advice. The following words and code are used on timetables and should enable you to decipher them confidently.

Key to timetable coding

PO-SA	Mon-Sat
Nepremáva	not on (dates listed)
Premáva	on (dates listed)
Crz	via
Okrem	except
Denne	daily
Školského vyučovana	school days
a	weekends
b	Mon-Sat, except on dates listed
c	school days
f	not on 24/12
g	daily except Sat
k	not on 24 or 25/12; or from 1/1-22/3

L	1/7-31/8 only
L5	27/12-3/4; 6/6-2/10
r	not on 31/12
u, w	school holidays
X (or ⚒)	Mon-Fri (usually shown as ⚒)
Z	12/12-30/6
†	Sun only, except for dates listed
6	Sat only, except for dates listed

FUNICULARS, CABLE CARS AND CHAIR LIFTS

Poland

See www.pkl.pl (English version) for full details of timetables and fares.

Slovakia

For the ***High Tatras*** see www.tldtatry.sk (English section) for timetables and fares. For the ***Low Tatras***, go to www.jasna.sk. The website for ***Malá Fatra***, www.lanovky.sk, doesn't have an English version but isn't difficult to use: click on 'Vrátna', and you should be able to tell whether the chair lift has reopened.

TRAINS

Poland

Polskie Koleje Państwowe (PKP), a state-owned company, operates services throughout the country. The only one directly relevant to this guide is that from Kraków Główny (Kraków's main station) to Zakopane. Full timetable information, in English, is available from www.polrail.com.

Slovakia

Train services are operated by the state-owned Slovak Railways. Timetables are prominently displayed at stations and are easy enough to decipher; note that IC (Intercity) and R (Regional) services are faster that OS (local, stopping-all-stations) trains. Departures are listed under *odchoy*. *Chodi v* (= in service) and *nechodi* (= no service) are two key phrases. The same information is available on-line at www.slovakrail.sk. This Slovak-only site is easy enough to use: under *Vyhl'adat' spojenie,* type in your departure station at *Odkial',* your arrival station at *Kam,* and the date under *Datum;* click again on *Vyhl'adat' spojenie,* and a full timetable will be displayed.

PICNICS

Picnic 1: See Walk 2 below.
Picnic 2: See Walk 3 below.
Picnic 3: Zakopane/Gubałówka funicular: see www.pkl.pl (with English version). Frequent departures from 08.00 (July-Aug) or 08.30 (April-June, Sept-Oct); barely 3min duration. Toilets, but no car park nearby.
Picnic 4: See Walk 4 below.
Picnic 5: See Walk 5 below.
Picnic 6: See Walk 6 below, but note: to avoid the lengthy cable car queue at Kuźnice, purchase ticket in advance at Orbis Travel in Ulica Krupówki (near the Ulica Kościuszki intersection); the fare includes the national park fee. The cable car runs from 07.30 (May/June, Sept/Oct). from 07.00 (July-Aug). The service is every 10min when it's busy. See www.pkl.pl
Picnic 7: See Walk 7 below.
Picnic 8: See Walk 11 below.
Picnic 9: See Walk 12 below.
Picnic 10: See Walk 15 below.
Picnic 11: See Walk 17 below.
Picnic 12: See Walk 19 below.
Picnic 13: See Walk 21 below.
Picnic 14: See Walk 20 below.
Picnic 15: See Walk 23 below.
Picnic 16: See Walk 24 below.
Picnic 17: See Walk 27 below.
Picnic 18: See Walk 27 below.
Picnic 19: See Walk 30 below.
Picnic 20: See Walk 31 below.

WALKS

Poland's Pieniny National Park *(see also page 40)*

Walk 1: Daily PKS buses from Szczawnica to Krościenko and back. (Note: There is also a useful 08.15 departure from Szczawnica to Krościenko only.)

Walk 2: Daily PKS buses from Nowy Targ to Szczawnica via Krościenko. Return on the same bus line from Krościenko to Nowy Targ, or catch a bus back to Szczawnica.

Walk 3: See Walk 2 above.

Poland's Tatra National Park *(see also page 50)*

Walk 4: Minibus to/from Strążyska Dolina. Catch one of the numerous private minibuses that provide cheap, frequent services between their base opposite the main Zakopane bus station and the main walkers' destinations, from at least 07.00. They do not run to a timetable, departing when they are full — or when the driver decides to leave anyway.

Walk 5: From Zakopane either take a regular PKS bus (lines 1 or 5, at least hourly, but up to 3 an hour from 1/6-30/9) or the private minibus (see Walk 4 above) to Kuźnice. Return by the private minibus from the end of the Strążyska Dolina road.

Walk 6: Travel to Kuźnice as for Walk 5 above. Return from Kiry either by regular PKS bus (the bus stop is on the main road) or by private minibus from the same stop. See notes about the Kasprowy Wierch cable car under Picnic 6 above.

Walk 7: From Zakopane either take a private minibus (see Walk 4 above) to Kiry, or a regular PKS bus: PKS line 57 operates daily, with approximately hourly departures; line 61 operates from 1/6-30/9 with the same frequency. Both PKS lines leave from outside Bar FIS opposite the main bus station. Return from Siwa Polana with PSK line 63 (approximately half-hourly) or by minibus from the same stop.

Walk 8: From Zakopane either take a private minibus (see Walk 4 above) or the regular PKS bus to/from Siwa Polana. PKS line 63 operates daily with approximately half-hourly departures.

Walk 9: Access as Walk 5 above; return from Kuźnice the same way.

Walk 10: From Zakopane either take a private minibus (see Walk 4 above) or the regular PKS bus to/from Polana Palenica. The relevant PKS services (lines 59 and 60) leave from outside Bar FIS opposite the bus station, with daily from 07.34 approximately every 15min.

Slovakia's Tatra National Park *(see also page 72)*

Walk 11: Trains from Poprad connect with the service to Štrbské Pleso via Starý Smokovec with approximately hourly departures. SAD buses provide a less frequent (and less luxurious) service, with 7 departures Mon-Fri and a few more during weekends and in the summer. There is also a SAD bus service linking Liptovský Mikuláš with the High Tatras area, via Štrbské Pleso, at least twice daily.

Walk 12: See Walk 11 above. The Solisko chair lift from Štrbské Pleso operates from 08.30-16.00, but double-check time of last descent.

Walk 13: See Walk 11.

Walk 14: See Walk 11.

Walk 15: Trains operate between Poprad and Starý Smokovec daily with approximately hourly departures. The equivalent SAD bus service has several daily departures, even more during summer and Sat-Sun. The Hrebienok

funicular railway operates a half-hourly service from Starý Smokovec, from 07.30-19.00.
Walk 16: See Walk 15 above.
Walk 17: See Walk 15 above for access to Hrebienok. For the return (and access for the Short walk): trains operate between Starý Smokovec and Tatranská Lomnica daily, with approximately hourly departures; SAD buses also link the two small towns daily and more frequently. The Tatranská Lomnica cable car operates from 08.30-18.30 (2/7-4/9) and from 08.30-16.30 (5/9-1/7). The Skalnaté Pleso/Lomnické Sedlo chair lift operates during similar hours, but check closing time before departing.
Walk 18: See Walk 15 above for services to Starý Smokovec and Walk 17 for Tatranská Lomnica. For this walk use the SAD Poprad/ Starý Smokovec/Tatranská Lomnica/Lysá Pol'ana service; there's a popular daily departure from Starý Smokovec at 08.50 and earlier departures during summer.
Walk 19: See Walk 18 above; use the same SAD service to go on to Tatranská Javorina and return from the 'Biela Voda' stop.

Slovenský Raj National Park *(see also page 98)*
Walk 20: See page 98 for the SAD Spišská Nová Ves/Čingov service; there is a stop just inside the national park.
Walk 21: SAD Spišská Nová Ves/ Hrabušice service to Podlesok: the bus goes through Hrabušice, diverges to Betlanovce and back, then continues to Podlesok; alight at a signposted junction where 'Autokamp' is to the left. Buses depart Spišská Nová Ves daily at 08.30, 11.15; return from Podlesok at 15.51. If you miss the 15.51, you will have to walk 2km into Hrabušice for a departure at 16.45 (weekends) or 17.25 Mon-Fri.
Walk 22: See Walk 20 above.

Slovakia's Low Tatras National Park *(see also page 107)*
Walk 23: SAD bus from Liptovský Mikuláš via the Demänová Valley to/from Jasná: 8 Mon-Fri (with some exceptions); 2 Sat-Sun; also 4 extra services in JulyAugust.
Walk 24: See Walk 23 above; alight at Záhradky for the Shorter walks. The Záhradky/Chopok Úboč chair lift operates daily from June to end Sept, from 08.30; check locally for time of last departure from Chopok Úboč.
Walk 25: See Walks 23 and 24 above for details of bus routes and chair lift.

Malá Fatra National Park *(see also page 115)*
Walk 26: SAD bus from Terchová to Chata Vrátna and return on the same line from Starý Dvor: at least 6 Mon-Fri; at least 3 Sat-Sun.
Walk 27: Bus as Walk 26 above; consult the tourist office in Terchová for information about the chair lift from Chata Vrátna.
Walk 28: See Walk 27 above.
Walk 29: SAD bus from Terchová to Štefanová and return, as Walk 26 (most buses to Chata Vrátna go via Štefanová).
Walk 30: See Walk 29 above. For the two Shorter walks take a SAD bus from Terchová to Biely Potok: 5 Mon-Fri (with exceptions), 2 Sat (with exceptions), 5 Sun (as listed in the timetable). Buses return from Biely Potok to Terchová with the same frequency (except that there are only 4 on Sun).
Walk 31: SAD bus from Šípková to Terchová: at least 5 Mon-Fri (with some exceptions) and 2 Sat-Sun; slightly fewer operate in the direction Terchová to Šípková.

Index

Geographical entries only are included here; for other entries, see Contents, page 3. A page number in **bold type** indicates a photograph; a page number in *italics* a map. Both may be in addition to a text reference on the same page.

Nowy Sącz
969
Połoczki
Krościenko
SCZCAWNICA
Pieniński Park Narodowy
Trzy Korony
Grajcarek
Dunajec
Červený Kláštor
Pieninský Národný Park
543
542
2
Podolínec
77
Tatranská Kotlina
67
537
Tatranské Matliare
Spišská Belá
Poprad
KEŽMAROK
67
Ľubica
LEVOČA
Starý Myln
18
Hôrka
E50
Spišský Štvrtok
533
Betlanovce
Hrabušice
536
Podlesok
Spišské Tomášovce
Smižany
Harichovce
Prielom Hornádu
Čingov
Hornád
4
Národný Park Slovenský Raj
SPIŠSKÁ NOVÁ VES

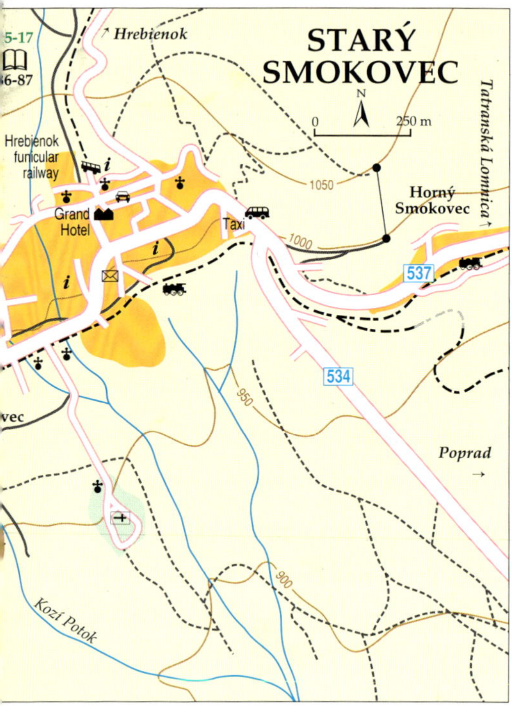
Hrebienok
STARÝ SMOKOVEC
N
0
250 m
Tatranská Lomnica
Hrebienok funicular railway
Grand Hotel
1050
Horný Smokovec
Taxi
1000
537
534
950
Poprad
900
Kozí Potok

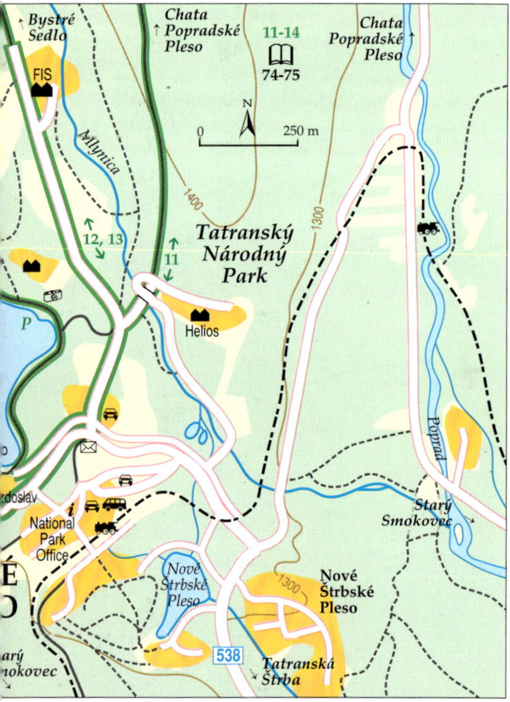
Bystré Sedlo
Chata Popradské Pleso
11-14
74-75
Chata Popradské Pleso
FIS
N
0
250 m
Mlynica
1400
1300
12, 13
11
Tatranský Národný Park
Helios
P
Poprad
Starý Smokovec
National Park Office
Nové Štrbské Pleso
1300
Nové Štrbské Pleso
538
Tatranská Štrba